The MILK LADY *of* BANGALORE

The Milk Lady
of Bangalore

An Unexpected Adventure

SHOBA NARAYAN

ALGONQUIN BOOKS
OF CHAPEL HILL
2018

Published by
ALGONQUIN BOOKS OF CHAPEL HILL
Post Office Box 2225
Chapel Hill, North Carolina 27515-2225

a division of
WORKMAN PUBLISHING
225 Varick Street
New York, New York 10014

Library of Congress Cataloging-in-Publication Data
Names: Narayan, Shoba, author.
Title: The milk lady of Bangalore : an unexpected adventure /
by Shoba Narayan.
Description: First edition. | Chapel Hill, North Carolina :
Algonquin Books of Chapel Hill, 2017.
Identifiers: LCCN 2017023398 (print) | LCCN 2017031072 (ebook) |
ISBN 9781616207618 (ebook) | ISBN 9781616206154 (hardcover)
Subjects: LCSH: Community life—India—Bangalore. | Cows—Social aspects—
India. | Milk—Social aspects—India. | India—Social life and customs.
Classification: LCC HM761 (ebook) | LCC HM761 .N37 2017 (print) |
DDC 390/.0954—dc23
LC record available at https://lccn.loc.gov/2017023398

10 9 8 7 6 5 4 3 2 1
First Edition

For Ranju and Malu,
who delight in telling people
that they own a cow.

"You can catch the tail of a cow and walk all the way up to the heavens," says the priest. *"That is why a cow is so important in Hinduism."*

—HINDU PRIEST, paraphrasing
from the Garuda Purana

CONTENTS

AYURVEDA CLASSIFIES MILK—AND EVERY substance, for that matter—not just on its taste (*rasa*) but also on its qualities (*guna*). This five-thousand-year-old indigenous healing system has analyzed milk in a dizzying array of ways and has come up with injunctions. Among them:

- Don't drink milk, which is a coolant, along with horse gram, which has heating properties. Not that you would impulsively come up with such an idea—"Oh, let's drink a glass of milk after chewing some horse gram"—but just in case you did.

- Don't drink milk after eating pineapple and sour-tasting fruits like berries. Probably because it will cause the milk to curdle in the stomach. I tried blending pineapple with milk. It didn't hold together.

- Warm, fresh milk straight from the cow's udder is like ambrosia. If you cannot for some reason drink raw milk, boil it. Drink it warm, not cold. Don't pasteurize or homogenize it. These processes help companies preserve and transport milk, but reduce the milk's intrinsic goodness.

- Young maidens should anoint their breasts with herbal butter to improve shape and size. Victoria's Secret, take note: maybe lace some butter into your push-up bras?

- Milk from a black-colored cow is best because it balances all the three *doshas* (imbalances) of the body. Milk from a red-colored cow balances *vata*, the air element that causes arthritis, gas, and bloating. Milk from a white cow is the worst: it causes *kapha* (mucus). What about milk from patchy black-and-white cows such as the Holsteins? Open to interpretation, I guess.

- Milk drawn from a cow early in the morning is heavier in consistency, since the cow has rested through the night. Hindu priests use this early-morning milk for their rituals and drink the lighter, evening milk after the cow has frisked around a bit. If you don't have access to a frisky cow, could you vigorously shake the milk can to simulate the effect?

- If you want to use milk as an aphrodisiac, choose milk from a black or red cow that has eaten sugarcane stalks. The cow must have given birth to a calf—but only once. It helps if the calf is the same color as the mother. The horns of the cow should point upward. The udder should have four nipples, not three. The milk should be thick, and the cow's disposition, calm. If you find such a cow, milk it in the evening; mix with honey, ghee, and sugar, and drink up. Have a nice night!

PROLOGUE

SARALA, MY MILK WOMAN, needs a cow. She tells me so when I chide her for giving me less milk one morning. It is 7 a.m. The school buses have left. I am standing outside my Bangalore home, waiting in line for fresh cow's milk. Sarala's youngest son, Selva, squats nearby, milking his mother's favorite cow, Chella Lakshmi.

I have known Sarala for ten years. I see her when I cross the road to buy milk. She asks me for many things but, so far, not a cow. Sarala is not sure how much a Holstein-Friesian cow will cost. She thinks it will be one thousand dollars or so. She has it all worked out. She will repay my loan through a supply of free milk—two liters daily, which costs about one dollar a day. Within a year "or two, give or take," the loan will be repaid, she says.

When I look dubious about her rate of return, she offers an explanation. "I need you to buy me more cows. How will you do that if I don't repay your loan?" she asks.

Then she lays it on thick. "You know, the family in the apartment below yours wanted to buy a cow for us. They like to do that, these Jains. Good karma, you see. But the timing didn't 'set.' When they were ready to buy, I didn't have space in my cowshed. When I had space in my cowshed, they didn't have the money. It didn't work out. You are lucky. Else why would I approach you instead of them when I need a cow?"

As a kicker, Sarala gives me naming rights to the cow that I buy—as long as the name ends with Lakshmi, the Hindu goddess of wealth. Otherwise, she says, the name won't set.

If you had told me years ago that I would write a book about cows, I would have done the "Elaine." I would put both my hands on your shoulders and push you hard, yelling, "Get *out*," as Elaine so often did to Jerry Seinfeld. In the late 1990s and early 2000s, I was a harried, working mother living in New York City. I liked dogs, not bovines. The only cows that I noticed were the wildly painted, acrylic sculptures of cows that had popped up all over the city, and those only because tiresome tourists would accost me on the street to have their picture taken in front of a pink or purple cow. Even then, I didn't link cows to India, the homeland I had left.

If you had told me then that this cow story would come to me, I would have laughed in your face. Not unkindly, but laced with a scorn I couldn't have hidden. Freshly graduated from journalism school, I would have said that waiting for stories to *come to you* was passive and fatalistic, so Old World. This was America, where you went after what you wanted, where you changed your destiny, made things happen.

I am older now and I don't have the boundless confidence of youth, the eternal sunshine of the unsullied mind. I realize now that opportunities sometimes present themselves in forms that you don't initially recognize as a story. I didn't know then how much Sarala, my milk woman, had to teach me about living in the moment and about framing misfortunes in a way that makes for resilience.

No, I didn't plan to write a book about my relationship with a cow. It literally walked up to me.

Cows are a cliché in India. They make headlines and are displayed on billboards. Sometimes, they eat billboards. They are the subject of parodies and exclamations, and like most stereotypes, epitomize an underlying reality: cows are indeed holy in India. Cows appear in the *Rig Veda*—one of Hinduism's oldest texts, written around 1200 BC—and in every Hindu text since. The cow makes an appearance in the magical and imaginative Purana (ancient) literature—whose stories encompass the collective myths and legends of a culture. Cows play many roles in these Hindu myths: warrior-princess, mother-to-the-world, primordial fertility goddess, fulfiller of all wishes, sacrificial mother, and harbinger of immortality.

The cow in India is a quagmire of contradictions and controversies, and also a symbol of the country's sometimes polarizing politics. That said, this is not an explicitly political book. It gives some amount of context about why the cow is so important in India. It isn't, and doesn't wish to be, a magisterial work on all aspects of the cow. Well, it sort of wishes to be a magisterial work on all aspects of the cow, but isn't one.

With these caveats, read on.

The MILK LADY of BANGALORE

Part One

THE COWS—AND HUMANS—
COME HOME

THE ELEVATOR DOOR OPENS.

A cow stands inside, angled diagonally to fit. It doesn't look uncomfortable, merely impatient.

I reflexively move forward, and then stop, trying not to gape.

"It is for the housewarming ceremony on the third floor," explains the woman who stands behind the cow, holding it loosely with a rope. She has the sheepish look of a person caught in a strange situation who is trying to act as normal as possible.

"Hey, hey," she shushes, as the cow fidgets. "Don't worry, the cow and I will get off on the third floor and send the elevator down." She smiles reassuringly.

The door closes. I pull out bug spray from my handbag, stare at it for a moment, and then put it back in. Does bug spray work against bovine germs?

I shake my head and suppress a grin. It is good to be back.

Although I grew up in India—in Chennai, or Madras, as it was then called—I left for undergraduate studies in the United States and didn't come back for close to twenty years. Returning to India was a long-cherished dream. Living here *is* like being in a dream sometimes, replete with surreal "only in India" sights, sounds, and smells that would have given Salvador Dalí either a ton of inspiration or a run for his money.

Like encountering a cow in an elevator.

OUTSIDE THE APARTMENT BUILDING, a large, red moving truck is parked near the curb. Two burly men are unloading cardboard boxes labeled "Crown Relocation." My husband stands on the sidewalk, checking off boxes from the list he carries: bedroom, kitchen, toys, and so on. Pink bougainvillea grows on the compound wall of the building named "Ivory." We are moving into a newly constructed apartment building named after a banned product created from elephant tusks that, quixotically, is painted in a shade called "ebony."

"You will never guess what I saw inside the elevator," I say.

There is no response.

"A cow."

Now he looks up, my husband.

"It is a busy time for cows," says the relocation guy. "A new building in Bangalore, many people moving in. They all want cows to walk through their homes."

Yes, I know what he means.

For Indians like me—equal parts global citizen and traditional Hindu—the role that the cow plays in Indian society, both as a symbol of Hinduism and as a reality that roams the street, is a matter of acceptance and embarrassment, much like what parents become to teenage children. On the one hand, Hinduism is intricately linked with this particular quadruped. On the other, you'd think that a modern democracy like India would get over this cow obsession already. What is the point of talking about software and IT and development if you can't cut off pastoral links with an ungulate that harks back to when nomadic tribes became settled civilizations?

Psychologist and professor Martin Seligman, often called the father of positive psychology, made a list of the six character traits that were valued by cultures across the world. The six traits, per Seligman, are wisdom, courage, temperance, transcendence, justice and humanity. In India, the cow is imbued with all these qualities in folklore, myth, and poetry.

Take justice, for example. The story goes that a king of the Chola dynasty, famed for its stunning bronzes that adorn museums across the world, hung a giant metal bell outside his palace. Citizens, he said, could pull on the bell's rope and summon him if they wanted justice. The king probably thought that it was a grand, if unnecessary, gesture. The rope was just for show, because who would have a grievance against his perfect kingship?

One morning, he woke up to see a cow pulling on the rope. Apparently, the king's son, the crown prince, had killed the cow's offspring under his chariot wheels. Mother Cow wanted justice. What would you do in this situation?

King Manu Needhi Cholan didn't offer the cow-mother a lifetime of hay as compensation. He didn't ask his son to go and apologize to the cow or to make nice. He ran his son down under chariot wheels—just like the prince had done to the calf. The son died, of course. Today, this king's statue stands at the entrance of the Madras High Court as a potent if largely ignored reminder of how the scales of justice ought to work.

My mother used to tell us about the "cow that rang the bell to seek justice." For a while after hearing this story, my brother, Shyam, and I tried ringing a bell in lieu of yelling an outraged "Mom!" when we got into a fight that needed an adjudicator.

Unlike the king, my mother ignored us.

A modern version of this tale plays out in the state I live in, Karnataka. It is captured not in ageless mythological manuscripts but on YouTube, in a video titled "Soul Touching Story of a Cow in Sirsi Asking for Justice."

The video shows a white cow that chases and stops a blue public transport bus in the town of Sirsi. We learn that her calf had been killed under the bus wheels weeks earlier. For five long minutes, in a honking, crowded Indian street, the cow stubbornly stands in front of the bus, looking below the bumper for her calf. A crowd gathers to stare at the cow; some people attempt to shoo it away from the front of the bus, while the bus driver turns the steering wheel to try to circumnavigate the cow. Every time that particular bus plies the road, the cow appears, we learn. Bloggers report that officials tried repainting the bus a different color. They even stopped its service for a few days to shake off the cow, but to no avail.

If myth is the smoke of history, as historian John Keay wrote, then some animals appear in its wisps more than others: the sheep in Christianity and the cow in Hinduism. India's link to the cow is both pervasive and perplexing when viewed through the lens of modern science. Do some Indians—not just Hindus—view cow urine as a cure-all? Yes. Do they use cow dung both ritually and in daily life? Yes. Do Hindus worship every aspect of the cow? Yes. Do they believe that the goddess of wealth resides in the anus of the cow? Yes. Are cows a symbol of growing Hindu intolerance and nationalism? Yes.

Ever since the Hindu nationalist Bharatiya Janata Party (BJP) took power, men posing as *gau rakshaks* (cow protectors) have assaulted Muslim and Dalit Indians. In September 2015, an angry mob of such cow vigilantes lynched and killed a Muslim iron-smith, accusing him of eating beef. In July 2016, cow vigilantes assaulted four Dalit men who skinned hide for a living. Muslims in India live in fear of these cow brigades who reserve their compassion for this animal at the cost of human lives. As for me, I love cows. I actually think that Hinduism's claiming them as an iconic symbol is pretty cool. But killing people for them? That is taking the sacred cow to a sacrilegious limit.

If you ask an Indian why cows are viewed as sacred in his country, he will probably say something like, "They herald good things." As a schoolgirl, I often saw cows with pink tassels around their horns being led ceremoniously into construction sites. A band walked in front, the cow walked next, and the construction crew followed, to break ground for the new structure. Inviting cows to warm houses is a tradition that continues in India. Fitting one into an elevator is a creative take on it. The Hindi word for this is *jugaad*.

Jugaad is makeshift ingenuity; improvisation; recycling, precycling, and upcycling; finding new uses for everyday objects—and for that matter, animals. Indians are masters at jugaad. It is the product of a resource-constrained culture. When you don't have enough, you figure out how to make do. You tie empty Coke and Sprite bottles around your waist in order to float in the water; you line up tattered shoes as goalposts when you play football; and you figure out how to get an animal to the third floor. But you don't give up on culture and tradition, particularly when they bring good luck. You don't give up on inviting a symbol of prosperity and good luck to walk through your home. You smuggle said symbol into an elevator. If it urinates during the course of this passage, you carry a bottle so that you can catch the urine, not because it will desecrate the place, but because cow urine and dung bestow good vibes on a house for complex reasons that have to do with ritual, tradition, habit, culture, and, yes, beneficial bacteria.

I used to be one of those "modern young people" who rolled my eyes and made snarky remarks about Indian traditions, particularly those that involved scatological remnants from ruminants. Now, I am not so sure. Early Indians found uses for cows and their by-products. Those traditions continue to this day. Beyond the milk, which is converted into yogurt, buttermilk, butter, cream, and ghee, there was the cow dung, which is used for cleaning courtyards of village homes and to make methane gas, or "gobur-gas," as it is called in India. The word *gobur* means "benediction from a cow." A part of me wants just such a benediction for my new apartment. The moving man provides the impetus.

"You should ask that lady to bring her cow through your home as well," says one of the movers. "After all, the cow is already in your building. She will give you a discount."

I glance at my husband. Before he says anything, before he

protests, I turn and walk back into the building. I ride up the elevator to the third floor.

The apartment door is open. Sandalwood incense perfumes the air. A colorful *rangoli* drawing decorates the floor. As is custom, mango leaves, considered auspicious, are strung together above the door. If you ask elders why mango leaves, they will say, "because it is tradition," or "because it is good luck," answers that can apply to any of the countless things that Hindus do. I suspect mango leaves are hung because they attract gnats and insects that will feed on the leaves and then forget about entering the house—kind of like leaving Halloween candy outside so that boisterous kids don't bother knocking on your door.

Outside the apartment stands the slightly fidgety cow with the woman beside her. "The cow cannot walk on marble floors," she says in explanation when I walk out of the elevator. "She will start skating."

Inside, the people, dressed in silk, are scrambling to line the floor with newspapers and old gunnysacks so that the cow's hooves will gain traction and not send her flying across the apartment. Finally, the floor is covered. The lady and cow gingerly walk in. A bare-torsoed priest begins reciting Sanskrit mantras. When they see me, the people smile with reflexive hospitality. A woman in a beautiful sari comes forward. She is clearly the mistress, beaming with pride for her new home.

"Please come," she says. "It is our housewarming. You are moving in upstairs, aren't you?"

I nod and smile.

"We are so lucky to have found a cow," she says, folding her palms prayerfully. "Now it is as if all the gods have come home."

"Amen to that," I say rather inappropriately. "All hail the holy cow."

My new neighbor stares at me, as if trying to figure out if I am joking or mocking. Probably both, even though I didn't intend to. "All thirty-three thousand gods live in the cow," she says huffily. "Her four legs are the Vedas; her eyes are the sun and moon; her neck holds the trinity. Even her dung holds Lakshmi, the goddess of wealth. *Gomaye vasathe Lakshmi; go mutre Dhanwantri.* Her urine contains Dhanwantri, the celestial physician. You didn't know this?"

I have a choice: to fudge and say that, of course, I knew every detail of her account. Or to tell the truth and say that I sort of knew what Hindu scriptures said about the cow without knowing the details.

"Of course, I knew," I say, a trifle too loudly. "That is why I came. I was wondering if I could hire the cow to walk through my home as well. After you are finished with her, of course."

The woman pauses and frowns slightly. I know what she is thinking. Will sharing the cow dilute the good luck that she hopes to accumulate?

"You could ask the cow's owner, I suppose," she says finally. "She sells milk to this neighborhood apparently."

I don't know my neighbor's name but we are already sharing cows. Our sojourn in Bangalore is off to a swimming start.

I nod at the milk woman. Her cow moos in response. Her name, I am told, is Sarala. The cow, too, has a name, but we haven't yet been introduced.

The priest calls my neighbor to minister to the cow, feed it sugarcane stalks and green bananas. She does so prayerfully, glancing at me every now and then as if to say, "See, this is how it is done."

A few minutes later, a young girl clad in a mango-yellow skirt hands me a bowl of milk *payasam*. "Please have it," she says. "My mother made it."

By now, I am convinced that this is my neighbor's ploy to show me up not just in the cow-hiring but in the culinary area as well. Or maybe she is just being hospitable. I nod my thanks and spoon up the warm, milky payasam. Flavored with roasted cashew nuts, it is sickeningly delicious. Much better than my uninspired version.

The priest calls everyone to feed the cow.

"Those who want the blessings of this goddess of wealth can feed it," he announces as we line up. I pick up my token, which happens to be fresh green grass. As we stand in line with our offerings; the priest recites some mantras. He explains their meanings to us.

"Daughter of Surabhi, the fragrant one, who is framed by the five elements of wind, water, earth, sky, and ether. You are, holy, pure, and benevolent. You have sprung from the sun and are laden with precious gifts. Mother of the gods, sister of the original progenitor of the world, and daughter of the ancient creators: the Rudras, Vasus, and Devas. Accept this food from me as a salutation to thee. Namaste!"

"Namaste," I intone just to blend in.

The cow stands in a dignified fashion and quickly eats everything that we offer. Her raspy tongue tickles my fingers.

After the cow is relieved of her official duties, I follow her and her owner as they amble out the door. Can she come up to the fifth floor and parade the cow through my apartment as well?

"Normally, they give me one thousand rupees [about fifteen dollars] for this, but since we are already here, you can pay us seven hundred," Sarala says.

We have a deal. I run up two flights of stairs while the cow and accomplice take the elevator. I feel that I ought to welcome the cow properly but there is little at hand in my empty apartment. I think about allowing it to lick my cellphone instead of a banana but decide against it.

"Welcome to the cow," I say formally as they come out of the elevator. My floor thankfully is not marble. It is red oxide and therefore rougher. The cow walks through my empty apartment, somewhat bemused and a little impatient.

"At some point, you should buy her some bananas as a thank you," says Sarala as she pockets the seven hundred and leads the cow outside. "Just as a gesture."

"That's why I gave you the money," I reply, wondering if she is negotiating for more cash.

"Yes, but cows can't eat money," she replies.

"Cows eat paper in India," I say. "I have seen them."

"Those are poor homeless cows, Madam," she sniffs. "Not my cows. My cows like bananas."

"So why don't you buy her some bananas with my money?" I have to ask.

"I will, but it has to come from your hand. Cows remember that sort of thing. The scent of your hand giving bananas will please her. She will know that you gave her a gift, you see? She will think well of you and bless your entire family."

"Does the cow know the scent of my hands?" I can't help myself.

"Oh sure," she replies. "A cow's memory is second only to an elephant's. It remembers everything and everyone. You just watch. When this cow sees you on the road, she will recognize you. She will shake her head, wag her tail, and bound towards you."

I am not sure if that is a good thing, but say nothing.

"Help me push her into the elevator, will you?" Sarala asks. "I'll go in first with the rope and you push from the back. The cow is used to wide open spaces, you see. The elevator is starting to freak her out."

I nervously follow the lady and the cow to the elevator. She asks me to put my hand on the cow's rear and gently push.

"But what if she poops on me?" I ask.

"That is a good sign for your house," she replies. "Do you know how many people give me a bonus to get the cow to poop in their construction sites? But what can I do? I cannot make her poop on demand. I have even tried feeding her extra sugarcane on the day before a housewarming. Sugarcane has lots of fiber, you see, but sometimes it happens and sometimes it doesn't. Just pray that she poops before she leaves. I won't charge you extra."

The elevator comes. I put both hands on the cow's rear and push.

"Don't touch its tail," Sarala says.

The startled animal sort of jogs into the elevator. It does not poop.

The doors close. I have sanctified my new abode with the cow. For reasons that I cannot put my finger on—that may or may not have to do with keeping up with the Joneses, or, in my case, the snarky neighbor who lectured me about holy animals—I am inordinately pleased.

The elevator doors open. This time, it is not an animal that exits but a human—my husband.

"What happened?" Ram asks. "You look happy."

I shrug. "I got the cow to walk through our house," I say. "My uncles will be thrilled."

"But not the kids. Don't tell them."

After Ram, the movers come, carrying large boxes filled with our belongings. Within moments, we get caught up in directing them to the different rooms. The boxes smell of New York—a potent combination of subway, hot dog, petrol fumes, and smoke. I gulp. What have we done?

2

BANGALORE

WE USED TO LIVE on Sixty-sixth Street and Central Park West, in the shadow of Lincoln Center. In many ways, it was an idyllic life. We walked across Sheep Meadow—had sheep ever grazed on that particular meadow?—to pet the animals in the Central Park Zoo. We woke up before dawn to move our car across the street depending on the day's alternate-side parking rules. We bought Priscilla's Pretzels from a cart down the street before ducking into the Museum of Natural History to see dinosaurs on winter afternoons.

I knew exactly which subway car to get into so that I could escape through the turnstile at the 116th Street station before anyone else in order to sprint up the steps to Columbia University's Journalism School when I was late for class. I knew the cashiers at Fairway, and could catch the eye of the baker behind the counter at

Zabar's—a decided privilege, particularly on weekends when the suburban hordes descended. He would nod slightly and throw me a box of chocolate rugelach.

We used nebulous words—culture, identity, and homeland—to explain the impending move to our friends, our two young daughters, and mostly to ourselves. Both Ram and I grew up in India. Though we became naturalized American citizens, we ate vegetarian Indian food at home and went to the Hindu temple in Queens. We spoke to our daughters in English and to our parents in Tamil. We have American passports but listen to Carnatic and Hindustani music. I watch *House of Cards*, *Homeland*, and *The Good Wife* rather than Indian soap operas; indeed I cannot relate to their high-octane histrionics, which make *Jane the Virgin* seem tame in comparison.

Exile, wrote Palestinian-born cultural critic and scholar Edward Said, is the "unhealable rift forced between a human being and his native place; between the self and its true home. It's an essential sadness that can never be surmounted." For immigrants like Ram and me, this is a double whammy. Born in India, we came of age in America. We could relate to both cultures, yet belonged to neither. We were like the primordial Trishanku of Indian mythology, who hung between heaven and earth, unable to choose his home. We straddled India and America, sandwiched between our Indian parents and American-born daughters.

Heritage is a hazy concept but that's what we used to explain our move to the children. We wanted them to know their heritage, we said, while hoping that they wouldn't ask if we knew it. The more tangible reason was our parents—both sets were still in India. They were getting old. Their annual trips to the States to spend time with us wore them out. We wanted our kids to know their grandparents, their cousins and relatives. After much heartache and discussion, we pulled the plug on our life in New York and moved to Bangalore.

HAVING MY BROTHER AND sister-in-law in the same city makes the transition easy. Their son and daughter get along famously with our girls. My sister-in-law, Priya, helps me figure out which schools to put my girls in. When they buy an apartment on St. John's Road, we decide to follow suit and buy a place in the same building. My parents live around the corner and so we recreate a new avatar of the old Indian joint family: both endearing and aggravating.

Across the street from our new building is a large army settlement, reflecting Bangalore's colonial roots. The British army was stationed in Bangalore, thanks to its temperate climate. We live in what's called the cantonment neighborhood, with the barracks now used by the Indian military and their families. Winston Churchill served here in his youth and still owes thirteen rupees to the Bangalore Club—a private club with a waiting list of thirty-two years for membership. Prince Charles offered to settle the account when he visited Bangalore in the late '80s, but the club, which proudly displays young Churchill's outstanding dues in a glass-enclosed ledger, refused.

The self-sufficient army enclave has schools, churches, clinics, homes, training grounds for its staff, and, as I come to find out, a milk woman to service their dairy needs. From our terrace, we look out at meticulously maintained roads bordered by flowering trees, clean sidewalks, and no garbage, all unusual for a large Indian city.

It is from this vantage point that I first see Sarala the cow-lady again. As I drink coffee at around six thirty in the morning, I watch army families enter and exit the campus. Cadets in khaki uniforms march out for training exercises nearby. Security guards are stationed at the entrance to ask if you are "phriend or phoe" (friend or foe), parroting a wartime instruction in a language that means little to them. Army wives clutch the hands of their children and walk them out to school buses. Civilians need to show a special permit, or answer questions before they are allowed inside. They can enter the army quarters to pray at the temple, church, or mosque inside, but that is about it. Cows and their caretakers, however, are granted a visa-free, no-questions-asked entry. The cows are led in to graze on the pastures that surround the barracks.

At the entrance is a cement culvert, about the length of a park bench. Here the milk woman sells her wares from a large, stainless-steel drum. Her cows are milked right there on the sidewalk so that her customers buy fresh milk straight from the source.

Three days later, I see her again. She is walking into my building as I am walking out.

"Got milk?" she asks. She is carrying a stainless-steel container filled ostensibly with milk. "Have you finished your *paal-kaachal* [milk-boiling] ceremony?"

Milk is the first thing that Hindus boil after moving into a new home. They allow it to froth, rise, and run over. The Hindu equivalent of "my cup runneth over."

"Yes, I have," I reply. "I used packet milk."

"Packet milk is inferior to fresh cow's milk," she says. "Just ask those army folks across your street."

"Do you sell your milk in my building also?" I ask.

"I'm carrying this milk for the new family that has moved in on the eighth floor. Do you want some?" she asks.

"It is very nice of you to ask, but no thank you," I hear myself reply with the exaggerated politeness people use when they want to shake someone off. With years of practice, Indians have a highly honed instinct for spotting artifice, power hierarchies, and the limits of negotiation. From across the room, in a crowded wedding hall, for example, people can zero in on another guest as a useful ally or useless loser. They might accost perfect strangers at the reception to ask if they know of any "good boy or girl" with whom they can forge "an alliance" for their daughter or son. There are subtle undercurrents that hinge on several questions that are occasionally at odds with each other: will she take advantage of me, or can I take advantage of her? Even if I take advantage of her, how can I preserve the relationship? How can I win this particular negotiation without pissing her off?

And on a daily basis: How far can I push the vegetable vendor/ milk woman/insert choice of profession into reducing the price of his goods so that I don't get scammed?

Raised in India and trained on the streets of New York, I am already a master of this. I know that the milk woman views me as not just a potential customer but also a potential marketer who will find her new clients in this brand-new apartment building of seventy families.

"My name is Sarala," she says.

I nod. I remember her name.

"You can find me every morning and evening across the street with my cows. We have been supplying milk for the last ten years. Ask anyone in the neighborhood. It is the best milk you can find. Here, have a taste."

She opens the container and waves it under my nose. Inside is frothy, white milk. Having drunk only pasteurized milk from plastic containers for twenty years, I am nonplussed by the earthy, grassy smell of fresh milk.

I shake my head. "No, thanks," I say. "But if I ever need it, I will come to you."

Sarala tells me that the army wives are tough, discerning customers who keep her on her toes. They demand the best milk, she says. You will get the same high-quality milk. You ought to try it, she says.

I nod distractedly. I have bigger problems to deal with—an elephant of a problem, to be precise.

RAM AND I HAVE joined the building's volunteer maintenance committee, taking turns attending meetings.

"We have a situation," Ram announces one day as he walks in after a meeting.

Apparently the German tenants want to hire an elephant to give rides at their daughter's birthday party. When our building committee refuses, they produce photographic evidence of a cow in the elevator. Since we have allowed cows into the building, why not an elephant? they ask.

Unlike our co-op in New York, our home here is part of a complex. There are three high-rise buildings arranged in a triangle. In the middle are a swimming pool, party hall, gym, and pool room. The entire complex is enclosed by a boundary wall. Around the towers is a driveway built to accommodate fire trucks but used mostly for walking or jogging. It is here that the German family wants to parade the elephant. There is only one problem: our parking garage is underneath the driveway.

No one on the committee is against elephants. In fact, it would be nice to get a ride on an elephant. The problem is whether our driveway can withstand the weight.

"The parking garage is a hollow space, which could collapse under the weight of an elephant," says Ram. "Heck, the whole building could collapse if the elephant walks on our driveway."

There is no way an elephant can be accommodated. What next, we think with outrage, but can't even come up with a bigger animal. We need a compromise. So we negotiate with the Germans. A horse is out of the question, they say. They have ridden horses in Germany. They need an exotic animal. What about a cow? we ask. There are plenty of cows around. The Germans look interested.

The committee deputizes me to approach the milk woman when they hear that I have interacted with her. My assignment is to make nice and secure one of her cows to give children rides around the building.

Now it is my turn to ask Sarala for something, and her turn to view me with suspicion.

"Cows don't carry people, Madam. They give milk."

What about bulls? She must have bulls in her stable of animals. After all, a cow needs a bull to fornicate and reproduce, yes?

She looks at me with pity. "Urban dairy farmers don't keep bulls," she says. "They rent bulls on demand. Most of the impregnation of cows is done through injection [artificial insemination] anyway," she says.

Can she find us a bull? I ask. The Germans will pay good money for the animal. There is a bull parked outside the post office down the road. I have seen it every day "with my own eyes," I tell her. A beautiful sleek animal with curved horns and a shiny white coat, loosely tied to the metal fence.

"Oh that," says the milk woman. "That's a Kangeyam bull. It belongs to the brick mason who lives behind the temple. It pulls his bullock cart filled with bricks. Would the children like to sit in a bullock cart? That we can arrange. Instead of the bricks, we pile on kids."

I am not sure. I have a feeling that the German kids would prefer riding a bull in the buff, as it were, sans bullock cart. They want it raw and real.

"What about a buffalo?" I ask.

Sarala shakes her head.

"Buffaloes are the vehicle of Yama [the Hindu god of death]," she says. "Why would you want children to ride death? Plus buffaloes are lazy. They won't carry children. Even if a crow sits on top of it, the buffalo lumbers."

"Can you find any animal that can carry children on its back?" I ask, desperate at this point. "It can be a cow, buffalo, or bull . . . "

The milk woman shakes her head. She knows people with bulls, but they won't carry twenty giddy seven-year-olds on a sugar high around the building. It isn't safe for the bull or the children. Bulls hate red. If a child wearing a red dress approaches, it will throw off the offending child and run away. Worse, it might bend down and ram its horns into the child.

"What about a tractor?" she asks. She can find a tractor with a trailer. All twenty kids can be given a single ride around the building. That is possible.

But that isn't acceptable to the German family. They want to send home photos of their daughter astride an animal, not merely sitting on a giant red tractor, the likes of which they can find back in Düsseldorf. They want an experience on the wild side, of true India. Finally, the maintenance committee agrees to let them use a camel for the birthday rides. How they find the camel is up to them.

A few days later, I encounter a camel when stepping out on an errand. It is a testament to German—and Indian—enterprise. A joint venture like none other. An Indian camel carrying German schoolchildren. I am not even fazed. I am getting used to India.

BANGALORE, NOW OFFICIALLY CALLED *Bengaluru*, has a population of about 12 million people. The city's booming economy has attracted some ten thousand expats and an equal number of foreigners who fly in every day for meetings with software firms and startups. In fact, if you only take in the glass-and-steel high-rises of South Bangalore and ignore the beggars, jasmine-flower sellers, squeegee men, vegetable vendors, transvestites, and of course cows, it is possible—difficult but possible—to imagine that you are driving through California's Silicon Valley. The buildings come quick and bold—Cisco Systems, Google, Hewlett-Packard, Microsoft, Sun Microsystems, Yahoo—and together they give this city its rather uninspired moniker: India's Silicon Valley.

In the beginning we all miss New York. The kids miss iceskating on the rink and the Christmas tree at Rockefeller Center, and their friends from school. I miss small things: stopping off at Isabella's for molten chocolate cake after walking through the Museum of Natural History; the sound of sirens at night; Ray's pizza, made with sauce, cheese, grease, and love; the breathtaking sight of the New York skyline from the Long Island Expressway; the crowds on Fifth Avenue during Christmas; the wispy smoke from vendor carts; the smell of roasted chestnuts, the fleeting sight of tulips in spring along Park Avenue; the clatter of the cash register at the Korean deli where I picked up milk on my way home; Jazz at Lincoln Center. Okay, I didn't actually attend Jazz at Lincoln Center very often, but it was nice to know that I could.

Slowly, though, we make friends and set down roots. We run into expats everywhere—or perhaps we seek them out. My yoga teacher, Javed, is from Iran; my daughter's piano teacher, from Hungary; and one of the reasons I go for a haircut at Talking Headz salon, on busy Brigade Road, is to get a jolt of stylist Seth Lombardi's Brooklyn accent. We go out for Italian, Mexican, Thai, or Japanese food—French and Belgian chefs headline five-star hotel kitchens here—and we can cook good Indian food at home now. The spices are readily available and they taste fresh, unlike the ones I got in Little India in Queens or at Kalustyan's in lower Manhattan.

Our kids adjust well. They like their new school and the fact that their very Indian and Hindu names—Ranjini and Malini, Ranju and Malu, for short—aren't mispronounced by their friends. They like the bone-rattling yet perversely exciting rides on auto-rickshaws. Basically taxis with three wheels, auto-rickshaws are my favorite Indian vehicle. Yellow and black, as iconic to Indian cities as the yellow cab is to New York, they are variously referred to as "auto rickshaws," "autos," "rickshaws," and, more fashionably, "ricks" by young people, as in "I'll just take a rick home."

In India, my kids succumb to the warm embrace of grand-parents and the pleasures of living in a land where everyone looks like them. They start making their own memories: tennis lessons in Cubbon Park, rollerblading in Coles Park, trekking in Nandi Hills, and going for Sunday brunch with friends at Garuda Mall.

Ram is the wildcard. He was head of emerging markets in Morgan Stanley with a portfolio of investments that went from "Chile to China," as he would say. How is he going to reinvent himself in a new land that, from a Wall Street–finance perspective, is still considered a developing economy—a backwater, to put it bluntly? Not to mention, a country of glaring inequalities. As it turns out, over the next ten years, Ram morphs into someone with fingers in many different companies that range from retail to micro-finance. The one who was most doubtful about our move back home ends up having the time of his life.

3

MILKING THE MILK STORY
FOR MY NEIGHBORS

EVERY MORNING AND EVENING, I watch the milking ritual that happens opposite my home with giddy trepidation. I fear for the health of my family but I am drawn to the novelty of getting milk from a known cow. Or perhaps it is just rebellion combined with a queer sense of being a pioneer: because nobody else in my building is trying it out, I want to. I will show them the way. When they see me and my family thrive on Sarala's cow's milk, everyone will patronize her, too. Eschewing "packet milk" for fresh raw milk: that is Shoba's Choice.

When I look up "drinking fresh cow's milk" on the Internet, the first site that comes up is fda.gov, followed closely by the Centers for Disease Control website. There is a ton of information about how bad raw milk is. In a video entitled "The Dangers of

Unpasteurized Milk," a maternal woman wearing a yellow sweater speaks in dulcet tones about the risks of raw milk: that it can cause diarrhea, vomiting, paralysis, and, in some cases, death.

The CDC website is no better. The jargon is so complex and scary that I stop my research. Instead, I look for cues where I live. The milk lady across the street has a line of customers, many from the army cantonment. They don't just show up; they wait in line for her milk. Apparently, they don't fall sick or die from drinking her cows' milk. In fact, the army people look healthier than the well-to-do people in my apartment building, all of whom get pasteurized milk from plastic packets rather than a live cow's udder.

Like many Indians, I grew up drinking fresh raw milk from a cow—and I'm perfectly healthy. In one generation, though, India has switched to pasteurized milk. Those who buy fresh milk from dairy farmers are in the minority. Yet even today, I know Indian families who live in posh neighborhoods with anglicized street names, such as Race Course Road, Boat Club Road, or Wallace Garden, in homes designed by internationally famed starchitects. Behind the Kartell furniture, Starck lamps, Roche Bobois modular sofas, and Frette linen—quite literally in the backyard—is a cowshed with a few native breeds providing milk for the family. You need a bungalow for this, of course, with a yard, where you grow hibiscus, marigold, jasmine, and roses for your daily *puja* (prayers). If you are unlucky enough to live in an apartment building, as I do, you have to improvise. (This is where jugaad comes into play again.) For me, Sarala, the milk woman, is it. And although years of living abroad have made me both suspicious of and entranced by this back-to-nature approach of my ancestors,

I am, perhaps without even realizing it, swimming towards such a life myself.

ONE DAY, I WALK across the street and strike up a conversation with Sarala. I tell her that I am considering buying milk from her but that I'm worried that fresh milk might be impure.

"How can you say that, Madam?" she replies. "It is the pasteurized milk that is impure. Milk curdles in a few hours. That is how nature designed it. How can it last in a carton for days?"

As proof, she invites me to a dairy wholesaler, where, she says, the milk that is delivered to homes such as mine is packaged.

We go back and forth for a week. I talk to her every day to convince myself that it is okay to buy her milk. She tells me about how milk powder is mixed with pasteurized milk to thicken the latter, about how pasteurization robs the milk of its essential healing qualities, and how nobody amongst her customers has ever gotten sick from milk.

"They may get diarrhea from the water but never from milk," she says.

Finally, I decide to bite the bullet and accompany her to see the wholesaler. Sarala says there is only one problem: We have to set off at 4 a.m. She needs to return by the 6 a.m. morning milking. The time actually suits me. At 6 a.m. I have to get the kids ready for school.

I set the alarm and go down into the 4 a.m. darkness. Sarala is waiting at the gate with a call-taxi, an Indian precursor to Uber for India.

The taxi driver takes off as soon as we get in.

"Careful. No need to go this fast," I mutter.

"He has to be done with us and get to the airport before the flights land," explains Sarala.

At Mother Teresa Circle near my home (and herein lies the irony—you'd think that people would drive more peacefully at a circle named after Mother Teresa), a milk truck comes flying down a side street towards our street. Our driver slows down but doesn't brake. Both vehicles engage in the macho brinksmanship that happens on Indian roads. Each expects the other to let him pass. Within moments, the inevitable happens, leavened slightly by the slow speed. Our cab hits the milk truck, which topples onto its side, sending about one hundred half-liter milk packets flying out on the street. They plop like water balloons and burst open, causing a spreading lake of white milk on the black tar road.

Our trip to the milk mart has resulted in a pool of spilled milk. Is this a sign?

"It is a good omen, Madam," Sarala says. "We wanted to see milk. The gods have sent us a milk shower."

Thankfully, nobody is hurt. The furious truck driver climbs out from the side of his vehicle and begins yelling at our unrepentant cab driver.

I survey the scene and wonder how we can get to the milk place and return in time to pack up the kids for school. I feel somewhat bad for thinking about my own concerns when the milk truck, engine still running, is spewing smoke from its exhaust pipe into the milk, making volcano-like bubbles on the road. The two grown men are yelling at each other, operating on the premise that a higher decibel level and attendant outrage means a lower level of blame.

A public transport bus appears behind us.

Sarala and I glance at each other. In unison, we get out of the cab, hail the bus, and hop on.

The two men are still yelling at each other over the spilt milk.

EVERY MORNING, WHETHER IN Kolkata or Delhi, Mumbai or Madras, India wakes up to the comforting plop of milk packets being deposited in front of homes. We scissor open these packets and make our masala chai infused with cardamom, cinnamon, ginger, cloves, and a pinch of salt. In the South, we make filter coffee, which is like café latte. We cut open a half-liter packet, heat the milk, and mix it with the coffee decoction.

The milk that comes out of these packets begins its life in a cow's udder. Or so we like to think. The milk makes its way to a wholesale center, like the one Sarala and I are heading to called Rajanna Dairy. The milk cooperative sits amidst a line of disparate shops: a Vodafone phone booth; a copy shop; a center that offers SAT instruction; and a chain bakery called Iyengar's.

We see dairy farmers leading cows down the dark streets and women clad in nighties carrying milk cans to the tiny storefront, which is a hive of activity. Cows stand at the cooperative's entrance, chewing on cauliflower stems that a vegetable vendor has discarded. Inside, each milkman squats beside his cow and collects the milk by hand in a stainless-steel bucket for sale to the proprietor, a paunchy man who stands behind the counter, collecting cash with rapid fingers. In the back of the store is a milk tanker with a cylindrical hold into which milk from the cows is piped. It will be taken to a giant pasteurization plant on the outskirts of the city, where the milk is heated, spun, cooled, and put into packets for distribution through the day.

Sarala greets the proprietor cheerfully. She tells me she sells her extra milk to him. He always gives her good prices. Her cordiality with him is at odds with her views on pasteurized milk. "I brought this Madam here to tell her about packet milk."

The man smiles. "When you are buying milk from Sarala, what is the need for packet milk?" he says. "Fresh cow's milk is best."

Sarala tries to egg him into saying that milk powder and other preservatives are mixed with packet milk. "Not here, of course. Not in your cooperative, but in other ones."

The man doesn't agree or disagree. "I have heard that such things happen," he says, counting money and disbursing milk packets with flying fingers. "But I haven't seen it with my own eyes."

Suddenly, a heated conversation erupts in the milking area out back. A farmer hasn't been able to track one of his cows. It was standing at the Cox Town Circle last night, he says He has been riding his motorbike all over the neighborhood since 3 a.m. Where could the cow have gone? It never leaves that spot.

People offer suggestions and sympathy. Perhaps the animal just wandered off into a bylane. Perhaps someone took it by accident. Perhaps the Muslim butchers have made off with the animal.

Why not register a police complaint, I say.

They all stare at me. I am getting used to this look. It says, "Look at this modern 'suit-boot' lady who has no clue about our lives and doesn't know what she is talking about."

They can't complain to the police, they say, because their cows roam the streets. The police will only take down an FIR (First

Information Report) and register a case if cows are stolen from
within someone's property. So these farmers buy Alsatian dogs to
guard the cows. They buy roosters to wake them up at dawn for
the milking; and then buy hens to give the rooster something to
do. Within the compound of an urban dairy farmer lies an entire
ecosystem.

DAYS AFTER OUR EXCURSION I am still waffling. I am avoiding
Sarala. She wants an answer; she wants it now and she has taken
my queasiness about her cows' milk personally. As far as she is
concerned, I have cast aspersions on the quality of her animals and
their milk. She is determined to prove me wrong.

"I don't want your business," she says one day. "It is not about
that. But you should realize that you are mistaken about fresh
cow's milk."

Sarala doesn't understand why I am hung up about pasteurization.

"No need to worry so much about nature's product," she says.

In the end it's the *idea* of buying milk from Sarala that I find ir-
resistible. Why do we love the things we do? Certainly it is not an
objective exercise. It is not even about taste. Raw milk, for me, isn't
really about taste. It is about ethos and to some extent principles—
principles that rest on a shaky foundation, I might add. If you swear
by wild-caught fish, grass-fed beef, or fair-trade coffee, you can find
a dissenter with a cogent argument that disproves your thesis. For
example, "Consuming wild fish caught in faraway rivers and seas
uses more fuel than raising fish on a local farm. Your insistence on
buying this product increases your carbon footprint."

The reason we choose an object, a product, or a lifestyle—whether it is mink or milk—has to do with complex layers of emotion, romance, nostalgia, and yes, if you must have it this way, loss. We buy mink because it reminds us of a happy childhood in Vladivostok with our elegant grandmother, a roaring fire, snow, and squealing, happy children. The reason I want to buy milk from a cow is because I am trying to recapture the simple times of my childhood, particularly after the intricate dance that I have undertaken for the last twenty years as an immigrant in America.

Milk is my way of reconnecting with the patch of earth that I call home.

CONVERTING MY FAMILY TAKES several weeks. My children refuse to drink milk directly from an animal. They don't care about implementing my farm-to-table, zero-carbon-footprint principles, which is what I tell them, even if the truth of why I want to buy Sarala's milk is more complicated. They want homogenized odorless Nestlé milk, with cavorting cartoon cows on the box, manufactured thousands of miles away in Zurich, and bought from Thom's, our local grocery store, where it is displayed—is there a message in this?—in the aisle next to laundry detergent and plastic plates.

Trained as an engineer, Ram, who graduated from the University of Michigan (imbibing its practical Midwestern sensibility) and worked with "quants" on Wall Street, is dead set against it. He says that we are inviting germs and bacteria into our home and bodies. My septuagenarian father-in-law is visiting and comes to my rescue. A rational man, he agrees that there are health hazards with raw milk. But he has grown up drinking raw milk from cows and knows that the pasteurization and homogenization processes rob the milk of its valuable digestive enzymes.

We come to a compromise. I will buy cow's milk but double-boil it, and then use it only to set homemade yogurt. The logic is that this two-step process of boiling the milk and then getting the probiotic bacteria to work on it during the process of fermenting it for yogurt will somehow beat down the malefic bacteria. The yogurt that we will mix with rice to make the famous South Indian "curd rice" will come straight from a cow. For our daily café latte and chocolate milk, we will continue to use homogenized milk from plastic packets.

Ram agrees to try it out for a month.

So one morning, I walk across the road with a stainless-steel milk can to buy milk from Sarala. We pay monthly. Each family purchases "milk coupons," at the going rate: some forty rupees a liter. If they need two liters of milk every day, as my family does, they buy sixty milk coupons, which, in Sarala's case, happens to be her business card with her name, address, and phone number. Each day, I hand over two business cards to Sarala for two liters of milk. Some families buy half-liter coupons, which is simply a business card in another color—blue, as it happens.

When my coupons run out, my milk woman replenishes them. There is no plastic involved. The cards are completely recycled, a system that satisfies me on many levels.

My simple act produces more reaction than I anticipate. I thought it was only my family who had opinions about my life and choices. Suddenly random strangers who watch me walk across the street with my milk can offer their views. People from my building tell me that Indian cows are sources of tuberculosis and other diseases, that I shouldn't buy their milk. Nina, the lady who walks her dogs in the morning, is among the dissenters. She issues dire warnings when she sees me buying milk from Sarala. Until that point, we are—quite literally—nodding acquaintances. She walks her cute pugs down the road at about the same time I take the kids to the school-bus stop. We nod at each other. That is it. Till the day she breaks our tacit cordiality with a single phrase: "I wouldn't do that. I wouldn't buy milk from those dirty cows."

It takes me a week to come up with a response. "What if your cows are dirtier than mine?" I say one morning.

"How do you mean?" she asks.

"Well, your milk presumably comes from a cow. How do you know that your cow isn't as mud-splattered as mine? How do you know that the cows that produced your packet milk are not tuberculosed, as you call it?" I say.

"Even if they are, the milk is pasteurized," says Nina.

It is her smug tone that does it. "Oh really," I say silkily. "Haven't you read news reports about milking plants experiencing power cuts, causing the pasteurizing process to stop halfway through? They take the milk to the point of curdling and boom, the power goes out and the pasteurization process stops." I am exaggerating wildly, of course, but the smug look is wiped off Nina's face. She looks distinctly worried. There are certain explanations that you can use with impunity in India—traffic jams and power cuts being two of them. I plunge in with the delicacy of an assassin.

"Haven't you read news reports about mixing laundry detergent with milk to give it girth?" I ask. "How do you know that your milk is properly pasteurized? How do you know that the stuff you mix with your coffee is not Tide, Shout, Surf Excel, or maybe all three?"

Nina has no answer. In her silence is my victory.

⁂

IT HAS ONLY BEEN a few weeks, but I have already become an evangelist for fresh cow's milk. One evening, to win over my neighbors and incentivize them to join me in my crusade, I invite several women to my home. My plan is to tell them about the cows across the street and see if we can start a milk cooperative. If a whole group of us "mass-affluent" citizens buys from my milk woman, we can pay her above-market prices and improve the quality of her cows (not that I agree with Nina the dog walker that the cows are diseased!). It will be like adopting a village, except we will be adopting some cows.

I invite these women, some of whom live in my building and some who live nearby, to come at around 5 p.m., in time for the evening milking. Instead of cocktails, I will serve them milk, or at least coffee and tea made with cow's milk. The proof will be in the drinking. Once they taste local cow's milk, they will change their minds forever. We will band together and collectively buy enough milk to give all the neighborhood cows good food and warm-water baths. Maybe we can create a cow spa with the extra dough. Our children will grow up feeling compassionate towards animals and predisposed towards eating and drinking local, seasonal food for life. They will escape obesity, diabetes, and every other ailment that troubles modern society, and live long and happy lives, thanks to the fact that we gave them organic raw milk. They will become champions of reducing climate change and the melting rate of glaciers. I have all the fervor of the newly converted.

It is a beautiful February evening. There is a light wind on my terrace. I arrange the chairs artfully in a semicircle facing the road, so that my guests can easily stand up and watch the cows being milked. There is music, canapés, and the clink of glasses. I think I might have made my invitation a tad formal, because the women come in wearing flirty cocktail dresses and silk saris. They have makeup, lipstick, and blow-dried hair. They have the look of women going out on a Friday night who are looking forward to pink cocktails interspersed with sparkling conversation. I decide to get the evangelical bit out of the way right at the beginning.

"Let's start with some tea or coffee," I announce brightly. "Who would like some South Indian filter coffee?"

My guests look wary—they had expected champagne—but play along. They all nod their heads, which is good because the milky coffee is already made. I serve each of them a small cup of coffee and invite them to the terrace. After a few moments of chitchat, I stand up and tap a spoon on my coffee cup.

"I have some wonderful news to share," I begin. "The milk in the coffee that you are drinking comes from the cows that are being milked right across the street from here."

Some of the women sputter and spit out the contents of their mouths into their cups. They look up and stare at me.

"We are living the California dream, my friends. People there yearn to buy local and organic. This is our version. Come," I invite. "Look at those cows down yonder. They are eating the grass that grows in our neighborhood parks. They are digesting all this with their four stomachs—not one, not two, but four stomachs. And they are giving out the goodness of their digestion in the form of the milk that graces your coffee." My voice rises.

When I rehearsed my speech, I believed that it would be touching. We would sip our coffee and commune with the mud-splattered but still-beautiful Holstein-Friesian cows who had given the contents of their stomachs for our coffee. We would stare down at them in silence and pledge to improve their lives and my milk lady's livelihood. We would be at one with nature and cows, and lead a zero-emissions life, at least in the dairy department.

What happens is a little different. Most of my guests immediately announce that they are late for another event. They have places to go. Some of them get emergency phone calls and have to leave right away.

I never see them again. Well, that isn't really true. Some of them live in my building and I am forced to encounter their baleful glares every time we pass each other at the gate. But it takes years before they agree to come to my home for coffee.

4

FARM TO TABLE, UDDER TO BUTTER

MY MILK ROUTINE SOON falls into place. I take my daughters downstairs every morning and wait for them to board the school bus at 7 a.m. Then I cross the street with a stainless-steel milk can to the culvert where Sarala and her cows stand. Typically, customers and I talk about schools and recipes, cows and garbage trucks, babies and bath water. A breeze ruffles our hair. Everyone is relaxed. It reminds me of the morning repartee that I had with our garage attendant, Chris, in New York. It lasted just a few minutes, while I waited for my car to be driven up from the underground garage.

"You a vegetarian?" Chris exclaimed one time. "Man, I would die if I couldn't eat meat."

"What's chicken like?" I asked

"Hmmm, lemme think. Like chewing gum," he replied.

"That sounds horrible. Why would you eat garbage like that?"

Friendly banter laced with mild insults. It is similar at the milking spot. We are a motley group from around the neighborhood. We can talk with an impunity that comes from anonymity. Beyond the milking, we don't socialize. Parakeets shriek joyously as they circle a fruiting fig tree nearby (*Ficus religiosa*). Milk from the cow's udder squirts softly and rhythmically into the large stainless-steel bucket. White bubbles hive the top.

Sarala herself is an engaging conversationalist. No matter what the situation, she has a comforting response. Shorn of false niceties and overt politeness, her speech brims with empathy and warmth.

"My son has so much homework," says one of the regulars one day.

"Why don't you change his school?" Sarala responds. "I did that for my son and it did wonders for his confidence."

"When was this?"

"Oh, thirty years ago. He is thirty-five years old now. Works with the Indian army."

"I am worried about my husband," says another. "He has gained so much weight. I think the military will throw him out of his job."

"Put him on a diet of millets and he will lose ten pounds in a week," says Sarala. "Make some *ragi* [finger millets] porridge every week. Just mix the batter with some onions and green chilies. Add a pinch of cumin powder. Chop up some curry leaves and throw them in. You've got yourself a tasty meal."

Three of Sarala's cows stand under the bauhinia tree, which has pink orchid-like flowers and leaves shaped like a widow's peak. One pink flower falls on top of a cow's head.

"Look, God just blessed this cow," exclaims Sarala. She walks up to the cow, touches its face, and then touches her head in a prayerful gesture. Others follow suit. Wanting to blend in, I do the same, even though I am internally frowning at what I think is a silly practice.

A fire-engine red BMW drives down our street, looking like Mardi Gras in a monastery. It stops across from us. A tall dapper man gets out, crosses the road, and approaches the cows. Everyone makes way, a little shocked by his three-piece suit. He carries bananas and holds them in front of the cow's mouth. The cow's rusty tongue swipes the fruit. The man puts his palms together and bows.

Sarala glances at me as if to say, "See, I told you. God has blessed this cow. Why else would she suddenly get bananas from a stranger?"

Wordlessly, the man walks back, gets into his Beamer, and drives away.

IN INDIA, SLUMS COEXIST beside sparkling towers. On one side of our apartment building is a five-star hotel, on the other, a series of slums. Sarala's home is in one of the slums and situated in a tiny gully beside a statue of Mother Mary. She has a loose arrangement for her cows: some stand guard outside her home, a few are fitted into a cowshed, which is at the end of my road and right beside a commercial milk parlor, and some roam the city looking for the bovine version of Airbnb.

"In the thirty years that I have lived in Bangalore, I haven't locked my house; not once," says Sarala. "I live with Muslims and Christians and we all help each other out."

As is typical of communities forced to live with each other in a ghetto, Sarala's view of other religions and castes is nuanced, specific, and sometimes opportunistic.

"These Muslims: they eat beef but I don't hold it against them," she will say. "You have a problem and they will be the first ones to offer assistance. They help me wash and clean my cows."

Sarala joins the Christians on her street during the annual St. Mary's Feast festival. She wears the beige sari that Christians don for a month and goes to St. Mary's Church in nearby Shivaji Nagar to pray. She thinks Mother Mary is more powerful than some of the Hindu gods she worships.

"You have two daughters. Why don't you prayer to Mother Mary for a son like Jesus?" she tells me.

I am used to the son preference of India manifesting in a variety of unsolicited questions and comments and have ready answers. "And have him nailed to a cross? No thank you," I reply.

Caste and religion are important to Sarala. Tending to cows, she says, is a Hindu occupation. Her husband's name is Naidu, a common enough name in South India. It also indicates that he belongs to the Naidu caste. Not all names are so transparent. My last name, Narayan, for example does not indicate my caste. I am what is called a "Tamil [language and region name] Brahmin [caste name] Iyer [subcaste name]." My cousin has converted his name to include an "Iyer" at the end of his name but I haven't. My relative in Massachusetts has anglicized the *Iyer* to *Ayer*, which is his current last name. Indians are adept at recognizing caste from surnames.

Naidu is a prominent South Indian caste. There is a shop named "Naidu Hall" in Chennai, which sells, among other things, great undergarments. According to Sarala, dairy farming comes naturally to Naidu folks. They have the touch. Cows trust them.

Sarala has a round face, soft clear eyes, and a beautiful smile. She looks like the cows she cares for, but I cannot tell her that. Relative to her withered, bald husband, she has the glow of youth, with shining mostly black hair and an unlined face.

"It is not simple, you know, to tend cows. These animals are very sensitive," says Sarala. "They can see what you and I cannot: one's past lives, one's aura, whether one is good or evil, whether a person is trustworthy."

"If they can see all these things, then why don't they run away from the butchers?"

"You think they don't try? What animal wants to die, Madam? Cows can outrun a man but they can't outrun a butcher's van."

Sarala, I am discovering, has answers for everything. She ought to have been a lawyer. Or a politician.

⁂

BANGALORE DOESN'T HAVE FOUR spectacular seasons like the American Northeast. Our seasons are muted but still felt. The Indian calendar identifies six *ritus*: spring, summer, monsoon, autumn, mild winter, and winter. Each season has a rhythm. Through the year, I get to know the rhythms of milking—both seasonal and daily. Cows get pregnant and need to be sequestered when sick or lactating, all of which we observe during the long sweep of the year. The daily milking, too, has a rhythm. It begins with herding of the cows, not on foot but on a motorbike. Selva, at twenty Sarala's youngest son, drives all over the neighborhood searching for his flock and nudging them with his bike so that they amble or trot to the milking spot. It is an urbanized version of a cowboy with his lasso. Selva knows where to find his herd. They like sleeping under the almond tree down the road, or occasionally foraging amidst the garbage for food. This, then, is the paradox of the holy cow: it is venerated but also allowed to forage amidst garbage. One much-cited documentary called *The Plastic Cow*, available on YouTube, shows doctors operating on a cow and removing 150 pounds of plastic from its rumen. When Prime Minister Narendra Modi chastised the cow vigilantes on national television, he said that those who care about cows should get plastic off Indian streets instead of beating up butchers.

Sarala doesn't believe that cows eat plastic. She thinks that the cows can pry open plastic garbage bags to access the vegetable and fruit peels inside. Not only that, Sarala says that they can discriminate, these cows, between vegetarian food and other meaty discards that they will not touch. I have seen cows nosing around garbage but I am not sure Sarala is right. Nor could she stomach what I saw in the documentary, so I don't bother trying to convince her.

By the time I come out with my milk can each morning, Sarala has already washed her large, stainless-steel buckets and placed them on the cement culvert. Selva hustles the cows to their milking spot, parks his bike, coats his hands with oil, squats beside them, and begins milking. On some days, Sarala's eldest son, Senthil, helps his brother herd the cows. But mostly, it is just Sarala, her husband, and Selva at the milking spot. Senthil is off doing "business," Sarala says. He tries many things. His current job is with a courier company. When we see him occasionally at the milking spot, he is astride a motorbike with a mobile phone. He zips away whenever he can on unnamed errands, something that Sarala rues.

"Can't even talk to that boy let alone get him to help with the milking," she says.

It is left to Naidu to manage the cows. While Selva milks one cow, Naidu herds the others to a grassy meadow just within the army campus. The meadow is about the width of a country road but enough to feed four free-range cows every morning. Sarala's herd has dwindled to ten cows, a decent number for downtown Bangalore, but she used to have more. "Look at me. When I moved to Bangalore, I had twenty-seven cows. Used to line them up inside the army compound and feed them. But my daughter-in-law does not have the cow-fortune. So my cow numbers are falling." Sarala has four sons. Only Senthil is married. She says that one of the things they look for in the horoscope of potential brides is *maatu raasi*, or "cow-fortune." Actually, Sarala vacillates about whether she wants brides with this cow-fortune. Yes, it will be good to find daughters-in-law who can take the baton from her and tend to the cows. Yet on the other hand, the whole world is moving away from cow herding. She wants her children to be happy and healthy, not stuck with cows if they don't want to be.

"As long as I am alive I will tend to these cows. After that?" she glances upward at the heavens.

Her husband has a different view. He sees cows as a livelihood rather than a life calling. Or so I think when I hear him complain about his wife. "Because of her, I am stuck with these cows," he says, nodding at Sarala. "If not, I would just sit in one place and take it easy."

"Yeah, right. He is going to sit still, it seems," snorts Sarala. "He can't even sit at home for one minute and the man claims he is going to retire."

They don't bicker much, though, this husband and wife. Too much happens; too much needs to get done. The cows intervene. Naidu has to go and tend to one that is mooing or stamping, or that needs to be untied.

"The man doesn't know what he is talking about," says Sarala after Naidu leaves. "The thing about keeping cows is that you won't fall sick. You have to wake up early and go to sleep early. You get good food to eat, good milk to drink, and the love of a good animal."

Sarala believes that, more than any other creature, cows are connected to humans. It is an emotional, intuitive bond, she says, that goes back millennia. Sarala likes all animals. But cows are special. When they live with you, they know how to give comfort, she says. "Whenever I am sad, I just go into the cowshed. A few minutes with these beauties and I forget all my woes," she says.

She loves and tends to them, and her cows return the favor. They know everything about their caregivers. They can gauge the future and foretell death.

"My grandmother had a beautiful, black cow," says Sarala. "One day, she slipped and fell. We all thought that it was a simple sprained foot, at the most a fracture. The ayurvedic doctor told her to take bed rest. We all went off to work. Not the cow. She came and stood outside my grandmother's window and began weeping.

Would not leave the place. For ten days, she stood there. That's when we realized that it was serious. Turns out that my grandmother had hit her head on the floor when she fell. Brain damage. She died twenty days later. The cow knew it from the beginning."

Cows may foretell death, but they also give life. When the gods and demons searched for the nectar of immortality, called *amrit*, they were told to churn the ocean of milk (*ksheera sagara*). A cow, Kamadhenu, sprang out of the ocean—as the harbinger of immortality. And it isn't just ancient mythology. A local folk tale tells of a cow called Punyakoti, meaning "millions of merits." The cow asks a hungry tiger to spare her life just for a few hours. I have a hungry calf at home, she says. Let me go back to my village, feed my calf, tell her that I will die, and then return to you. Ha, says the tiger. Like I believe that. The cow promises. I never go back on my word. Ask anyone. Finally, the tiger relents. The cow goes back to the village, feeds her calf for the last time, and tells the other cows to take care of her young. After a weeping, bleating farewell, she returns to the tiger, who is shocked that this cow has kept her word. Rather than kill any more beasts, he jumps off the cliff and commits suicide.

The Sanskrit word for cow is *go*, and cows are venerated as Gomatha, or "Cow-mother." Cows are maternal, for sure, but they can also be warriors, saints, martyrs, and mistresses. In the Ramayana, a mighty king, Vishwamitra, appears with his army at the hermitage of the sage, Vasishta. The king and his army are stunned to see a huge banquet laid out with fruits, milk dishes, and sweets, all of which are given by the wish-fulfilling cow, Sabala. The king wants the cow. No way, says the sage. The army tries to take the cow by force. The cow vanquishes the army by turning into a bovine fighting machine. She emits arrows and spears from her horns, burning coals from her tail, conjures up a variety of fighters from various parts of her body. She wins against Vishwamitra, who abdicates his kingdom and does penance to become a sage.

German Indologist Hermann Jacobi explains why Hindus venerate the cow in an essay printed in the *Encyclopaedia of Religion and Ethics*, a sprawling series of books published in the 1920s. He writes that Hindu belief in the sanctity of the cow "seems to have been inherited by the Indians from prehistoric times, before they and the Iranians had separated." Which is another way of saying that the earliest Indians originated in Iran. These Indo-Iranian tribes called themselves Aryans, from the Sanskrit word *arya* (a designation indicating nobility, honor, and respect). These nomadic herders crossed over the Hindu Kush Mountains to encounter the Indus Valley Civilization in the plains of what is now Pakistan and Northwest India. Once these Aryans settled in India, they wrote the four Vedas, Hinduism's earliest texts, and hence came to be called Vedic Indians. Vedic Indians were Hindus. Christianity, Judaism, and Islam came much later to the continent. Today, not all Indians consider the cow holy; only the 80 percent Hindu majority does.

The "Go Suktham" ("Verses on the Cow") in the *Rig Veda* begins simply: "For our health and welfare, let the cows of all ages, sizes, and progeny come and stay in our home." For Hindus, the cow epitomizes compassion and goodness, offering a veritable cornucopia of life-giving products that promote health and healing.

Prior to their passage to India, the Aryans, or Indo-Iranian tribes, worshipped a divine being called Geus Urvan, or Goshurun (literally, "the soul of the cow"), who is regarded as the personification and guardian of living beings according to Jacobi. This belief in the sacredness of the cow persisted as they moved into a new continent. And persists amongst a large portion of their descendants to this day.

SARALA THINKS THAT HER COWS are keeping her family happy. "These young girls—my daughter-in-law, for example—don't realize that, Madam," she says. "They don't understand the importance of the cows, and what they give to the family. They want to work in an office."

As she talks, Sarala walks amidst her cows, scratching behind their ears. Her voice is soft and soothing.

"What do you do?" she asks about a year after we have met.

"I am a writer."

"Do you make a good living?"

"Good enough."

"How much salary do you get?"

I pause. In India, I am used to intensely personal questions. I don't necessarily want to reveal my income to my milk woman.

"Not much. All my salary goes to pay off my home loan," I say casually.

Sarala nods sympathetically. "Just drink some warm milk. You will feel better."

For Sarala, the road to salvation is paved with warm milk.

Sarala means "easy" in Sanskrit, but her life is anything but. Like many of India's 200 million poor, she is beset with troubles. On any given day, she has to deal with alcoholic men, absconding sons, leaky roofs, or a constipated cow.

It is this last problem that comes to my attention one morning. I stand in front of the line, vessel in hand, and watch Selva milk. A few army wives are trickling out of their quarters to join the queue. The normally placid cow is shaking its head and making weird snorting noises. I gaze into her beautiful, distressed eyes. It is obvious that something is wrong.

"She won't urinate," Sarala says. "I think she has piles."

I nod. Can a cow have piles? And is that connected to non-urination—or the liquid version of constipation, anyway?

Sarala clears her throat. "Do you have any spare cash?" she asks. "I need to take her to the doctor."

"How much?" I ask.

She wants one thousand rupees, or about fifteen dollars. It isn't a lot of money but it is, I know, the beginning of a loan cycle that will never end. Seeing me hesitate, Sarala quickly adds, "I'll give you free milk till I repay the loan."

I loan her the money. How can I say no? This is India, after all. Cows are sacred. And she does give me the free milk till her loan is paid back.

5

THE MYTHS AROUND MILK

Is it because we begin our lives with milk? Is that why milk is considered sacred in several cultures, not just in Indian culture? The Greek goddess Hera spilled her breast milk and created not a wardrobe malfunction, but the Milky Way. When her husband Zeus lusted after a beautiful maiden called Europa, a jealous Hera turned Europa into a white cow and drove her into the continent that bears that name and made the term *cow* into an epithet to be forever used by jealous women and angry men. Not a woman to be trifled with, our Hera.

The Old Testament mentions the "land that floweth with milk and honey" over a dozen times, always in a positive way. Judaism prohibits milk and meat to be mixed or eaten together. The Koran contains a passage about the origin and importance of milk: "And surely in the livestock there is a lesson for you . . . " The Ramadan fast is traditionally broken with dates and a glass of milk.

Milk is part of cultural slang ("to milk someone").

"The milk of human kindness," wrote Shakespeare in *Macbeth*.

"As pure as milk," goes the expression.

Well, perhaps not so pure anymore. Milk has become a minefield with respect to nutrition. Current medical literature blames milk for everything from iron deficiency and colic to Type 1 diabetes and some kinds of cancers. Vegans believe that milk poisons the body. Most ancient cultures believed the opposite. They got their protein from milk and its byproducts. The Turkish salty sheep's-milk cheese *beyaz peynir* and the Indian cheese *paneer* both hark back seven thousand years to when Neolithic populations attempted to tap the high nutritional punch of milk by converting it into easily digested cheese. Indian literature views milk as a benign super food. Ayurveda touts milk products as calming and healing. Elders sometimes fast by consuming nothing but milk or they break a strict fast with a glass of milk.

Priests perform rituals on a stomach empty of all nourishment except for milk, which is okay to drink. It is above ritual, above rules, and all about faith. Ritual offerings of milk and yogurt are customary in Hindu temples.

Religion is filled with animals of all sorts, not just cows. White horses, such as Pegasus, feature prominently in Greek, Celtic, Slavic, and Indian mythology. Birds abound: as messengers, soothsayers, and predictors of good or bad events. But cows are imbued with particular qualities in Indian mythology. They nurture and save humans. They exude a certain patience, an acceptance. Some have said a "maternal acceptance." But I know that motherly acceptance is mostly an oxymoron. Mothers can be cheerleaders and champions but they also push and nag in ways that are the opposite of acceptance. Mothers are annoying—I say this as both a mother and a daughter—and not necessarily accepting.

Sarala is a tranquil and calm mother. I can tell. Her sons circle around her like moons. Their chronic lack of money hasn't cleaved the family apart. Quite the opposite, in fact. A dozen people live in Sarala's one-room tenement: she and her husband, Naidu; their first son, Senthil, and his wife; their remaining three sons (one of whom is not her biological son but was born to her cousin; Sarala has raised him); and her brother's family of four. Her brother married a first-cousin and they had "slow children," says Sarala. It had to do with their blood group being Rh positive.

"We didn't know at first. But when the first child was born, we could tell that something was wrong with him. So, we roamed around from hospital to hospital seeking help so they could have more healthy children," says Sarala. "Short of a full blood transfusion for my brother, the doctors said that they could do nothing. We couldn't afford blood transfusion. We told my brother and sister-in-law to abstain. But how can you stop God's will? My sister-in-law got pregnant again. What could we do? We prayed to God and left it all in His hands. Their second child was a daughter; a beautiful girl. She is . . . " Sarala shakes her head and purses her lips. "She is the same way, too. My brother almost went mad when he had these two children. He started drinking and, even now, you can find him lying near a ditch—completely drunk. My sister-in-law stares into space like she is dead. But what can you do?"

Sarala took in her mentally disabled niece and nephew along

with their parents. The kids are ten and nine years old now, she says.

"Do you know any special school that will have them?" she asks. "At least for a few hours so my sister-in-law can go and work? How will she feed the family otherwise?"

Sarala's frequent requests used to irritate me. Now, I merely exhale and nod.

Yes, I say. I will look for a special school for her niece and nephew. I keep it in the back of my head. I know that Sarala won't hold me to it, that she won't even bug me about her request because there will come another crisis in her life and she will move on from this one. To her, friendship is about the sharing of woes. She vents to me about her life and listens to me with empathy.

The thing is that Sarala has a porous sense of self. She would help me if she could and asks for help when she needs it. The notions of personal space and boundaries are not so meaningful to her, living as she does with a dozen people. Sharing information and assistance is part of who she is. The army wives constantly ask her for advice on healing through herbs—*naatu vaidhyam*, it is called, or "country medicine."

One day, she brings an egg curry that she has made for a pregnant army mother. "It will give you warmth during this cold winter," she says.

When I complain of a backache, she shows up at my doorstep with what appears to be white, wobbly custard. "One of my cows just gave birth. This is the first milk of the cow. It will give your back strength," she says.

Turns out that the sweet milky substance that Sarala has given me is colostrum, the first milk that a cow feeds its calf. It is filled with nutrients and antibodies.

Sarala assures me that she isn't depriving the calf. "We only take a small amount of leftover, after the calf has drunk its fill," she says.

I take the stainless-steel container hesitantly, not wanting to offend her. Sarala has told me that it is sweet and that I should just swallow it like custard. I don't feel like eating a cow's colostrum.

When our cook, Geeta, sees the dish, she gasps. "Do you know how hard it is to get this?" she asks. "Dairy farmers in the village charge a lot for this dish. It is like gold. To think that she gave it to you for free!" There is respect in Geeta's eyes for my milk woman.

The colostrum signifies a change in our relationship. There is a lot more give and take. When I casually mention that I have guests for dinner, Sarala throws in an extra liter of milk, no charge.

ON SOME DAYS, I follow Sarala into the army compound. As a civilian, I am not welcome there. When I accompany Sarala, however, I am waved inside. We go in together, one evening, before the milking. One of her customers has told Sarala that there is some fresh grass growing on the far end of the campus. Under normal circumstances, Sarala would lead her cows in to eat the grass, but they are barred for a few days because the military rookies are laying a new pathway and don't want to be bothered by cows trampling and shitting all over their work. So she and I walk into the sunset, searching for the spot. In her hand, Sarala has a scythe, a beautiful instrument with curved teeth, perfect for cutting grass.

Children play in the spacious playground, about the size of a city block—a luxury in space-starved Bangalore. Two army wives in caftans sit on their stoop, chatting. We talk with them for a few minutes and then find the lush patch of grass. "Look at this," Sarala croons. "My cows are going to be so happy."

With even strokes, Sarala uses her scythe and cuts the grass for her cows. "Poor things! They stand outside, looking at me with large eyes, waiting for fresh grass. This will invigorate my babies."

As she works, she points out a variety of greens: one that is good for the eyes, a creeper that alleviates pain in the knee joints, and a leaf that will bring down blood sugar if chewed. "For every disease, nature has created a cure in its leaves and plants," says Sarala. Within minutes, she has pulled a variety of wild greens and set them beside the bale of fresh grass.

"Take two red chilies," says Sarala without preamble, as she usually does when she gives me her recipes. "Two cloves of garlic, a piece of ginger. Nicely wash the greens, chop them up. Sauté the greens in a little oil. Garnish with some cumin seeds. Eat it hot with rice and ghee."

"Are you sure?" I ask. What if these greens are poisonous? Will I die?

"Why are you getting scared?" Sarala says scornfully. "Would I poison you? I take these greens and make them for my family. Because you are my friend, I am giving them to you."

I ask her what she is making for dinner. She has asked her daughter-in-law to mix some dough for rotis, she says. She plans to chop up some cabbage and mix it with the dough. They have guests and she needs to whip up something special.

"Are they here for long?" I ask.

Sarala nods. A week.

I raise my eyebrows. A week is a long time in their busy lives.

"What to do, Madam?" says Sarala. "We only seem to get guests who stay for long, not the kind who leave quickly."

We talk desultorily. It is lovely. The setting sun is still warm on our backs as we squat on the earth. In the distance, I can hear the screams of joyful children. A brahminy kite (*Haliastur indus*) swoops low to the ground. It is looking for snakes, Sarala tells me. The raptor's eyes are like binoculars. It can zoom in on snakes from a mile high. The trees sway gently in the breeze. Barbets, Asian koels, parakeets, and blackbirds chirp all around.

"It is so peaceful here," I tell Sarala.

"Come in the morning and do some rounding [walking around] of the field like these army wives do," she urges. "It is good for health. You can sleep on an expensive bed stuffed with money and cover yourself in a designer velvet bedspread. All that is useless if you don't have health. Walking amidst these trees will give you good health."

"The guards won't let me in," I reply.

"Tell them you want to go to the temple," says Sarala, pointing to the tiny temple in the premises, where a group of ladies is sitting and singing *bhajans*.

I am remarkably relaxed. As relaxed, I would like to say, as I am with a good friend. But the truth is that Sarala is not my friend. We spend time together, but there are large chunks of her life that I know nothing about and there are entire chunks of my life that she is unaware of. She and I have a bond, though, the shape of which is evolving. My conversations with her are so comfortable because they are wrapped in genuine affection and because they are without agenda. Then again, this is not true. We have agendas, Sarala and I. Hers is to figure out what she can use me for, whether it is to find a special school for her niece and nephew or find more customers for her milk from within my building. Mine is to figure out how to learn as much as I can from her. At the end of the day, though, I cherish my relationship with Sarala. With Sarala, I can let my mind expand. I can say the first thing that comes to me without fear of judgment or retribution.

That night, I try Sarala's recipe. The greens are soft and juicy and not bitter at all. Warmed by the sun, protected by tall grass, pulled out of the earth by the expert hands of my milk lady, and carried across the compound by me straight from earth to fire, they are the best greens I have ever tasted.

Sarala introduces me to new and wondrous things often. The patch of land that is the holding ground for her cows before and after their milking is home to bees, butterflies, shrubs, and plants, each of which has its own use and purpose. When I get a skin rash, Sarala plucks off a few leaves from a nearby plant, rubs it in her hand to warm it, and then squeezes out the juice. The thick green liquid smells vile but soothes my skin when she applies it, drop by drop. Within a day, the rash is gone.

On some days, Sarala brings different varieties of greens from within the army compound. On others, she shows me spiders and spotted owlets that make their home in the craggy bauhinia and flame-of-the-forest trees nearby. Casually and without fuss, Sarala opens my eyes to the urban Indian network that has been right under my eyes yet remained invisible so far.

Cows are the epitome of patience in this community network. Goats are tetchy, arching their necks stubbornly against the rope as they get pulled down the streets. Roosters scratch the ground moodily. Stray dogs are hyper—racing each other, chasing their tail; cats, aloof; and crows, clingy. Cows wait their turn. Their eyes look at eternity. As animal species go, cows have a good temperament. Not all of them—the Tapti Khillar cows that can outrun a horse across ravines and rock formations are like moody, bad-tempered divas—but most cows are pretty even tempered. They have to be in order to adjust to the urban environment. Cows aren't fazed by traffic. They amble right through or simply stand or sit.

One of Sarala's best milkers often falls asleep right beside the road divider. I ask Sarala if she is worried about her cow getting hit by traffic. She shakes her head. Who will hit a cow in India, she asks?

I don't believe her, and with good reason, as I will find out. One day, I watch a cow standing in the middle of the road. Vehicles race by: dozens of rickshaws, trucks spewing diesel, buses overflowing with people, cars of every stripe, bicycles with school children riding side saddle, standard issue bullock carts, scooters with two riders and a goat straddled between—the usual cross section of traffic in India. They all come hurtling down and screech to a halt before swerving crazily around the cow while somehow managing to avoid each other. Not once does the cow get hit; nobody comes even close.

Since then, I have observed cows ambling across highways, sleeping at night on roads, and lying beside the median on busy streets. These animals are nuts, I think. Or worse, dumb. They are inviting death. But it doesn't seem to happen. It is the traffic that swerves to avoid the cow.

"Why is the cow so secure on Indian roads?" I ask Sarala.

"She is like your mother. Who will run over their mother?" she says.

When I don't look convinced, she adds, "She is the giver of wealth, of prosperity. Why would you kill the goose that is laying golden eggs?"

I nod, surprised that Sarala knows that story. She takes my silence as disapproval.

"You have to shoo them away, Madam. Why don't you do that?" Sarala accuses, taking the offensive. "When I see cows by the divider, I pick up a stick and shoo them over to the side. These animals don't know any better. They don't have as much brains as us."

"I thought you said that they are as smart as humans," I mutter.

She is contradicting herself, but I get it. It is an age-old question: are animals smart? Are dogs smarter than humans? Are cows? Depends on what parameter you use. Their sense of smell and spatial memory are probably far better than ours. But anticipating accidents? Maybe not.

I think of Sarala's instructions every time I see a calf or cow sitting in the center of the road. The only problem is that it is hard to stop my car, get out, find a stick and shoo the animal away. There are too many vehicles honking behind me, their size inversely proportional to the volume of the horn. Mopeds trumpet like elephants; motorbikes roar like lions; my massive SUV that can fit ten people has a wheezy horn like a geezer's cough. They all drive like maniacs but never seem to hit the animal. Is that fear of being cursed by Mother Cow, compassion for the mute bovine, or an ancient instinct that teaches humans to value livestock?

As my father, an English professor, notes, the word "cattle" comes from the Latin *capitale*, a term that referred to moveable personal assets. Walking bovines were moveable assets not just for hunter-gatherers but also for Sarala's ancestors and mine, not to mention Sarala herself.

Early humans domesticated cattle in two places. The *Bos taurus* species was domesticated nine thousand years ago in the Fertile Crescent, the strip of land that runs from the Nile River Valley through the Middle East to the Persian Gulf. The *Bos indicus* species was domesticated in the Indus Valley region in Baluchistan (in modern-day Pakistan) between 6500 and 5000 BC. Until then, wild aurochs about the size of Indian lorries (midsize moving trucks in America) had roamed the world and been immortalized seventeen thousand years ago in the cave paintings of Lascaux.

Domestication may have emerged as a solution to overhunting. Dorian Fuller, professor of archaeobotany at University College, London, writes, "Each step along the trajectory, from wild prey to game management, to herd management, to directed breeding, may not have been guided by a desire to completely control the animals' life history but instead to increase the supply of a vanishing resource. In this way, animal domestication mirrors the process of unintentional entanglement associated with plant domestication as humans first foraged and then, through increased reliance on the resource, became trapped in positive feedback cycles of increasing labor and management of plant species that were evolving in response to human innovations." Humans and cattle came together, with each dependent on the other. Sometimes, after killing animals, humans took in their young and nurtured them as pets. Large males were hunted because they had a higher amount of animal protein, leaving the smaller males to mate with the females, thus selectively and perhaps inadvertently breeding smaller-sized cattle over several generations. Docility and adaptation were prized and selectively bred, leading to the taming of the shrewish aurochs into the docile cows that we see today. The wild auroch went extinct when the last one died in Poland in 1627. Now there are attempts to resuscitate them through genetics.

The *Bos indicus*, known as zebu or hump-backed cattle, is characterized by a fatty hump above the shoulders, folded dewlaps, droopy ears, and more sweat glands than their European cousins. In India, they are simply called *desi* or "native cows." These cows can handle hot, humid climes. The Indian food chain, even in busy urban cities, still links cows and humans. In my home, for instance, I boil cow's milk every morning, then let the milk cool a little before scooping out the cream on top and setting the remainder into yogurt. I collect the cream for a week and then churn it to separate the butter from the buttermilk. I divide the butter into two parts: one for sweet cream butter to spread on my children's toast and the other to boil into ghee or clarified butter. The whole thing is a painstaking process—a nuisance, really—but I do it. As do many of my neighbors. We set yogurt, churn butter and when needed, squeeze a bit of lemon juice into the milk to curdle it into fresh paneer. Doing all this is a daily reminder of all we get from a cow, the giver of good things.

SARALA'S SON SENTHIL HAS a baby boy. Sarala wants to name the baby—her first grandchild—Muneeswaran, after their family deity, but the family is worried that the name will sound too old-fashioned. They want a modern name—short and snappy, like a Bollywood hero.

"It has to have two syllables, Madam," says Sarala earnestly. "Only then will companies give you a job. If my grandson goes and says to an IT company that his name is [she sings this out] *Moo-neee-swaaa-raaaan*, they will tell him to milk cows, not man a computer."

Finally, the family reaches a compromise. The baby will be called "Muneesh," modern enough for Bangalore and expandable to "Muneeswaran" when they visit aging relatives in Sarala's native village of Arni.

Senthil quits his job at the courier company to start his own business selling bottled water. I see him now and again, carrying large bottles of water on his motorbike.

"Why don't you ask those rich people in your building if they will buy my son's water?" Sarala asks me often. "He has the best water; better than Ganga water. And he will come and deliver it at your doorstep."

"Okay, Sarala," I say.

She knows I am brushing her off.

"Why don't you try bottled water for a month, Madam? Our Kaveri river water is so bad."

"We use a filter at home."

"Oh, you shouldn't trust those filters. They don't remove all the dirt. Better to drink bottled water."

This from a woman who uses a plastic sieve to remove the stray germs and flies from her cow's milk.

Sometimes Sarala brings Muneesh to the evening milkings, and the customers take turns holding the baby. Sarala wants a grand-daughter. After four sons, she is fed up with boys. "Girls take care of us in our old age," she says.

Then she adds, "Keep your eyes open for a good school for my grandson."

6

ARE YOU HAPPY?

HOW WOULD THE HAPPINESS studies that put India low on their lists explain the resilient matter-of-factness of India's poor? Happiness studies call it adaptation. People get used to a certain standard of life, a way of being. They adjust to their lot. They learn to be happy within their means. Are they happy? Yes. In part. Well, most people are happy in part, you could say. But in India, the swathe of what is acceptable is broader. Notions of poverty are wider. Sarala's healthcare woes spiral out of control each time someone in the family gets sick. Much of her family is illiterate.

Money is linked to happiness: not just in India but all over the world, even though not all rich people are happy—quite the opposite sometimes. But the reverse isn't necessarily true: not all poor people are unhappy. Most studies use self-reporting to measure happiness. They ask questions and use the answers to gauge the person's "subjective level of well-being." This is a ridiculous approach in my view, because Indians—or for that matter most people from Eastern cultures—have been trained not to share or even vocalize their good fortune, in case someone casts the evil eye and jinxes it.

Ask a street sweeper if she is happy and often you will get the sideways shake of the head that means, "Yes." Or she will reply with obliqueness.

Question: "Are you happy?"

Answer: "Where is the scarcity for happiness?" ("*Khushi me kya kami?*")

Nobody in India would have the following exchange, which I regularly had in sunny Greenwich, Connecticut, where we once lived.

"How are you today?"

"Fantastic."

In India the best you'd get is "could be worse."

The Gallup World Poll and the World Happiness Report use Princeton social psychologist Dr. Hadley Cantril's *ladder of happiness*, in which people imagine their "best possible life" by answering the question "On which step of the ladder do you personally feel you stand?" Indians would reflexively choose the lower steps. What if you climb so high you topple off?

Which may be why the World Happiness Report 2016 ranks India 118th among 156 countries, below Somalia, Bangladesh, China, and Iran. Yet other studies throw a monkey wrench in the India happiness quotient. One study, conducted by Robert Biswas-Diener in the slums of Kolkata, reported high levels of well-being even though income levels are low. Part of it has to do with acceptance and contentment, avoiding what happiness researchers call the "hedonistic treadmill." Carol Graham, a fellow at the Brookings Institution, calls this the "paradox of happy peasants and miserable millionaires."

I don't know how true that is, but the pain of India, at least for me, has been to learn how to deal with the inequalities of life that I see between my family and the people who help us in our house. I know these are among the top attractions for most expat Indians who contemplate moving back to India: they can afford to pay staff to help with raising the children and keeping house. But being fundamentally egalitarian in principle and approach, I view things differently.

Every now and then, my American friends will ask me, "What is the hardest thing about living in India?" Some things in my list are trivial and random. I miss a good bagel, good wine at a decent price. But for me, being surrounded by people whose means are drastically different from mine opens up a Pandora's box of guilt—and it bothers me. We have a fantastic cook at home. Two sisters come to do the "top work," as it is called in India—sweeping, mopping, doing laundry, washing dishes, cleaning the bathrooms. We have a driver. Four people to take care of the four of us. It is ridiculous, actually.

But these encounters also give texture to my life in Bangalore. It begins at dawn and doesn't stop till late at night—when the ironing man comes with my freshly ironed clothes as we finish dinner. Then the other milkman, Shiva, who brings our pasteurized milk in packets. He works for a moving company during the day but wakes up at 4 a.m. to collect milk packets from the local dairy union to sell to customers like me for a small profit. The newspaper man, Nagaraj, is tall and athletic. He delivers newspapers and works at a courier company during the day. I have two flower vendors: Shafi delivers flowers in the morning and Mastaan in the afternoon. At least, that's the arrangement. Sometimes, both of them deliver strings of jasmine in the morning. Our two maids come in and out of the house. As do the driver, the gardener, and the handyman.

These are the people I see daily. They know my life and I know a little bit about theirs. Most of the time, our interactions are brief. Sometimes, they take on an urgency, which happens when they need money and ask me for it. That's when I get to know them as people. I know their concerns, their lives, their personalities, and their ability to pay back large loans. That's when India knocks on my door.

Sarala wakes up at 4:30 a.m. every day. Her herd is spread all over the place: a couple in the cowshed down the road, four tied in front of her home, and another four wandering around the neighborhood. Sarala washes the four cows that stand in front of her home, cleans their dung, gives them breakfast, and sends them on their way by 5:30 a.m.

Sarala brags about her cows. "They have an unerring sense of direction, these cows," she often says. "They walk straight to the milking spot."

She makes it sound like they have GPS tracking, when in fact her home is just down the road a few blocks away. But still, the cows find their way to the milking spot, lending credence to the notion that they have great spatial skills and memories.

Typically, Sarala's cows walk themselves from their cowshed to the milking spot opposite my apartment building. These are the holy cows that roam Indian streets, the ones that drive-by tourists photograph with their cameras. The same cows that make me angry because they are a danger to themselves—and others—on the roads.

What most people don't realize is that these cows have a biological urge and a purpose that drives where they go. In the morning and evening, they walk with steady gait and patient faces to a specific location for a date with their destiny, to relieve themselves of the milk that has collected in their udders. During the day, in between milkings, these free-range animals search for grassy patches in India's urban jungle. If all else fails, they dip their noses into garbage and eat vegetable peels—and, as we know, sometimes plastic, too. Cows don't want to eat garbage, says Sarala. They have adapted to their urban lifestyle. They know where they can find leftover vegetables.

Instead of cows, I get two humans cleaned and fed, and send them on their way to the school bus every day with a pat on their back.

I wake up at 6 a.m. and get half an hour of morning calm before the yelling begins.

"Take a shower."

"Hurry up, we are going to miss the bus."

But the magical time from 6:00 to 6:30 is mine. It is light outside. Sunrise comes early to South India. Typically, I open my balcony door to listen to the sounds of the koels and kingfishers that frequent the jacaranda trees around us. I love this part of my day. Hot coffee and me on my balcony. A black kite has recently built a large nest on an adjoining silk cotton tree. She has used leaves and twigs, but also Styrofoam and mop detritus, adapting the tools to her urban dwelling. I watch this kite every morning using my

binoculars. She sits on her three white eggs, unmoving and quiet
for hours: an act of profound maternal warmth.

One day, the morning breeze is uncharacteristically warm when
I open the balcony door. Immediately, I know that something is
wrong: there is too much noise, the sound of people shouting in
the ashy dawn.

I walk out on my terrace and look down. It is a horrifying sight.
A cow lies sprawled on the road, its legs bent at an unnatural angle.
There is so much blood. Yet it is alive and in agony. People appear
out of nowhere, as they do in India. It is one of Sarala's cows. The
security men at the army gate know it. Someone is charging down
the road towards Sarala's home.

A crowd gathers around the bleeding cow. The few vehicles on
the road stop. Some people pull over and join the crowd. Others
move on.

For a few seconds, I stand completely still on the terrace. I have
a clear view. That is the problem. Blood. So much blood. Like a
river. Why isn't the cow dying?

I don't want to go down.

"I'll be right back," I tell Ram and go down.

Sarala, Naidu, and Selva come running. They are carrying gunnysacks. The crowd closes ranks like the closing of lotus petals for
the night. I can tell that they are lifting the injured animal on the
gunnysack. They pull it to the side.

I stand outside my gate. Part of me wants to cross the road and
console Sarala. But the vegetarian in me stays rooted to the spot.
Thankfully, the crowd hides the animal from my view.

Sarala is wailing. I cannot make out her words but I can hear
her pain.

The men beside me are talking. There is the mechanic from the bike shop next door, the ironing man who takes my clothes and gets them ironed (not dry-cleaned, just ironed), the security guards from my building, the watchman in the bungalow down the road.

A garbage truck hit the cow, I learn. It swerved in the darkness to overtake a bus and didn't see the cow standing on the road. The driver didn't stop. Sarala, Selva, and Naidu are in the midst of a crowd of people. Everyone is talking, offering opinions. The onlookers want justice; they want compensation.

Sarala's family wants that, too, but knows it is a futile quest.

"Hard to find the garbage truck driver who hit and ran. He would have washed off the blood from his vehicle and parked it back."

"Even if we find the driver, what is the use? The animal is dying."

"How will the driver pay for the dying cow? He is probably a poor man, too, like us."

"The government has to pay," says someone.

"Why will the government pay? They will say that it is the cow's fault. Or the milk woman's fault for allowing her cows to roam on the streets without a leash."

"Why don't you call the doctor?" I yell across the road.

Sarala cannot hear me.

"No use, Madam," says the security guard next to me. "The animal should have been spot-out [died on the spot]. Its legs are gone. How will those folks afford a surgery to fix its legs? And even if they do get leg surgery, the animal won't walk properly. It will become a liability for life."

Thoughts fly around my head. What should I do? Should I call a vet? I don't know any vet. Should I call Sarala's vet? I don't know his number. Should I pay for surgery? How much will it cost? Will it work? Should I get involved? Maybe I can get the vet to at least put the animal out of its suffering.

"Tell her that I will pay to help the animal," I yell.

One of the guards runs across the road, cuts through the crowd, and conveys my message.

A teary Sarala crosses the road. Through the crowd, I can see the animal. It is still.

"Look at our bad fortune, Madam. The cow has just given birth to a calf. So unfairly, he has hit it and gone."

"Call a doctor. Let us call a doctor," I urge.

Sarala shakes her head. She has already made some calculations. "The doctor can't do anything. The cow is dying."

"Why not try?"

She shakes her head again. "Too late," she mutters.

Her stubbornness is crazy.

"Why not kill it then?" I say, hoping that I can get a stronger reaction rather than mere resignation.

Sarala looks shocked. "How can we kill it, Madam? We are just praying that it dies soon."

She walks back across the street. I don't accompany her. I turn around and go back into the elevator. Filled with useless rage and sadness, I snap at my family. What should I have done? What could I have done?

The cow dies—on its own. It took half an hour but at least they didn't have to kill it. "I just held its head on my lap and stroked it, Madam," Sarala tells me tearfully an hour later when I come out again. "Naidu wanted to strangle it but I didn't let him. Why play

God? One of the army men offered to shoot it. I couldn't allow him. What if the cow miraculously survived? What if the bleeding stopped on its own? Then at least we could have tried to get splints for its legs or looked at some *naatu vaidhyam*."

Selva hired a truck to transport the carcass to the butchers. They paid him some money for the animal, he tells me. He needed the money for cow feed. One of the other cows is going to calve anytime.

"Have you insured your animals?" I ask Sarala, though it's probably the wrong time to bring it up.

She scoffs. "All that is for rich people like you. For poor people, God is the only insurance."

The street-cleaning ladies are helping Sarala wash the blood off the road. They bring buckets of water, toss it on the blood, and scrape it with coconut-thimble brooms. The bloody water rushes to the side where it is absorbed into the drain. The bloodstains are visible for days, and indeed months and years—for those who know to look for them.

Sarala has a high fever when she shows up the next morning. Her face is puffed up from the crying. Her eyes are bloodshot. She can't speak. Naidu and Selva are more composed but they, too, can barely talk. All of us are quiet.

Selva squats on the ground, milking a cow. I awkwardly place a hand on his shoulder and crouch beside him.

"It is okay, Selva," I say.

I remember what I have heard my parents say during condolence visits. "Your late husband will get reborn as your grandchild. Don't worry, at least he got to see his son married and meet his daughter-in-law."

I adapt it. "Don't feel sad, Selva. One of your cows is calving soon. The cow that died will get reborn as this calf."

"What to do, Aunty?" he says. "I don't think I can eat beef anymore." He pauses and amends. "For at least a month. After seeing all that blood."

I am speechless. Because they care for cows, I had assumed that Sarala and her family were vegetarians. Then, I think to myself: that's like expecting every animal-loving farmer not to eat meat.

Sarala walks up to us. "He is very attached, this boy," she rasps. "What to do, Madam? It is our misfortune. Bad time."

"It will change. You will get another cow," someone says. "For all the good service you are doing for these cows, God won't let you down."

"That cow's *ayus* [life span] was short. God wanted to take it away."

"Maybe some big *gandam* [obstacle] was to hit your family and affect your grandson. The cow absorbed all those evil vibrations to save your family. It died for you; on your behalf," says the lady standing beside me. "It sacrificed its life for you."

"My mind is all *bejaar* [messed up]," says Sarala.

This is how they talk, the urban poor who grace my home and life; their speech is as hard and abrupt as their lives, leavened by a humor that sprouts "like a lotus in a dirty mud pond," as an oft-quoted Tamil proverb says.

7

EMBRACING HUMILITY, HUMANITY . . . AND GUILT

"Do you want to milk a cow?" I ask my younger daughter, Malu, who by now is ten.

"Yes," she says. Malu says yes to everything. Unlike her older sister, a teenager, who has learned to say no.

I don't remember what prompted the milk discussion. Maybe it was a documentary we were watching. Or maybe it was my reading about Michelle Obama instructing the White House staff not to make her daughters' beds so that they could grow up doing chores.

So we set off one morning, Malu and I, to milk the cows across the road. Malu is clad in shorts and T-shirt from Target. We are in high spirits. Look at me—just like Michelle Obama, I think with a glow. She makes her kids make their beds; I make mine milk a cow. Both of us want to keep our children grounded. My plan is to throw my daughters into the deep end of India: in deep dung, if it comes to that.

We cross the street to milk Sarala's most gentle cow. The plan is to wait till everyone has left with their milk before trying our experiment. To our surprise, Sarala is holding a calf's rope loosely. We coo over the brown calf. It is not yet used to humans. Malu gingerly strokes the calf's forehead. The calf backs away.

"Hey, hey," Sarala says in the scolding voice that her entire family uses when talking to cows.

It used to bother me in the beginning to hear Selva, Sarala, and Naidu chide the cows into submission.

"You have to talk to them like that," says Sarala when I ask her why she is constantly admonishing her cows. "These cows are too smart. They can guess who is boss in an instant. If you give them a little room, they will take charge and be the boss."

The calf tries to take charge by nuzzling its way towards the milk. Sarala holds the rope in an iron grip.

"Look at her. So greedy," says Sarala admiringly.

Malu is excited and very nervous.

Selva stares at us, completely baffled: this giggling mother and daughter. I have already coaxed him into letting us try milking.

Selva gives us a bottle of oil. Rub it on your hands, he says.

We stare at the grimy bottle but do as he says.

Our bodies are not as flexible as his. We are unable to squat on the ground like he does. In our honor, they have placed a dirty upturned bucket beside the cow. We go near Chella Lakshmi, the chosen cow. Sit, Selva commands. Malu sits cautiously on the upturned bucket. The cow stamps and swings her tail, which hits Malu. She screams.

"Why are you screaming? She is only swatting flies," says Sarala in the same scolding voice, a shout really, that she uses with her cows. It sounds like a rebuke. To my shock, Malu calms down immediately.

Selva squats beside Malu. Without a word, he rubs the cow's teats with oil for a minute, squeezes and pulls; squeezes and pulls.

Malu glances at me as if to say, "You do it first," and abruptly gets up from the bucket.

I take a deep breath and sit down gingerly. I touch the cow's teat. It swats me. I pull back.

Sarala brings the calf near the cow. "Sometimes these cows can be so stubborn," she says. "They'll hold back their milk and only let it down when they see their calf. Especially the new mothers. They won't let us milk till their calf has been fed."

"But this calf isn't this cow's child, is it?" I say.

"No, but it is better than nothing," Sarala replies. "Go on, do it."

I squeeze and pull. To my delight, milk squirts out. Not a lot. Still, it comes out. I glance at Malu before continuing the motion. A small stream of milk falls down into the bucket placed under the cow's udder.

Selva stands beside me, judging my performance with a frown of concentration. "You are pressing her teats too hard. She will clam up," he says. "You have to massage and coax her to give her milk. It isn't an abrupt pull like how you are pulling. It is a sweeping, massaging motion."

All these instructions are making me nervous. I must have

pressed too hard or pulled too hard. Whatever the reason, the cow lets out a huge volley of dung. It splatters on the ground. Small pieces ricochet off the ground and land on Malu and me.

My ten-year-old screams like she has been shot. I grab her and move to one side. The cow shakes its head and takes off. The stainless-steel milk bucket topples on the ground. Thankfully, it is nearly empty. The little milk inside it pours out on the ground. Out comes a small mouse from a hole in the sidewalk. It slurps up the milk. A crow flies down to sip on the milk.

Malu stares at the receding back of the cow, the rodent, and the crow. She is speechless. Selva has taken off after the running cow. Sarala comforts the calf that is distressed that its proxy mother is running away.

"Look at that mouse. Isn't she cute?" says Sarala, attempting to soothe and encourage Malu. It has no effect. Malu insists on going home and taking a shower. I send her back home and ask Sarala about the calf's mother. Why didn't she bring the calf's mother to the milking spot?

"That is the cow that was run over," says Sarala matter-of-factly. "This calf is an orphan. I am trying to get the other mothers to accept her and give her milk. One of the other cows has adopted this calf and loves to give her milk. But Chella won't take in a new-comer. If she accepts this calf, though, the calf's future is secure. Because you see, Chella Lakshmi's milk is the best."

Playing matchmaker between orphaned calves and cows is the hardest part of her job, says Sarala.

LIKE SARALA, NOBODY WHO works for me has any savings. One sickness can set them back. If my cook Geeta's husband gets sick, she has to go pawn her jewelry to get some money. Geeta came to me the other day. She is a warm, dramatic woman. My children adore her. She needed to borrow a significant sum of money, she said.

"Madam, my landlord is troubling me. Can I get two thousand dollars as advance?" she asked with the flair of a thespian. Once, Geeta said that she felt like taking rat poison because she and her husband were having marital issues. Her life is one of high drama. There are the usual problems: power cuts, no water supply, leaking roofs, and visiting relatives who expect to be fawned over even though she is a working woman who really doesn't have the time for it.

"Last week, remember, I had to take a day off to stay home because the whole clan showed up? I felt like my head would burst," says Geeta. "Coming to work here and relaxing is one thing; staying home and dealing with all the attitude I get from my sisters-in-law is torture."

Yet she is a cheerful worker, no different from a professional in an office, except a whole lot poorer. Though she won't take my chocolates, one day she comes in with her own bag of treats. "Madam, my son passed second standard. Here, have some sweets—for joy."

Part of it is practice. When life is hard, you figure out how to cope. You develop reflexes. Take Shafi, my flower man who delivers strings of jasmine every day. He is a Muslim who knows every Hindu holiday and chooses appropriate flowers for each. Shafi is always smiling. I mean that literally. It is unnerving. He was smiling when he told me that he couldn't deliver flowers for a week because his brother died. Is that a defense mechanism, mere politeness, or is that his nature?

The rickshaw driver who I hail one morning for a half-hour ride to the mall speaks to me pleasantly about the state of politics and cricket. I casually ask him how many children he has. "Five," he says. Of which four died at birth. Oh, God, that's terrible, I say. "Yes," he says politely. "But I am going to make my remaining son a big man. Educate him. Make sure that he has a real job, not just drive a rickshaw."

Is grief a luxury that the poor cannot afford, caught up as they are in the business of making ends meet? It is clear to me that Sarala loves her cows. Yet, the way she and her husband deal with the recent death of her cow (and livelihood) is very different from what I would expect. Over the next month, she talks about it often, each time with a different explanation as if to make sense of it in her head.

Sometimes one of her customers will tell another the story about the fateful morning. "One of the cows was ambling in the middle of the road when a corporation truck that tried to overtake a school bus hit her. Bystanders pulled the fallen, bleeding animal to the side of the road and called Sarala."

I glance at Sarala's face as the story is being recounted. She blinks rapidly.

"I think I must have done some horrible thing in my past life. Don't know why the good Lord took away one of my babies."

One of the army wives nods towards Sarala. "Poor thing, she is not eating much. Wasting away," she says to a fellow customer—a new customer—who looks shell-shocked and horrified at the tale.

Sarala nods and smiles reflexively, as if trying to assuage the newcomer's distress.

"What to do, Madam?" she says. "We shouldn't have allowed our cows to wander the streets. Who can we blame? Our planets are not aligned. Our time is not right."

They tried to revive the cow, she tells the newcomer. Tried calling a doctor even (they didn't). But nothing could be done. The cow's leg was gone. How to keep an animal without legs? That would be cruel. They had to "let her go."

"Can't you complain to the city government? That one of their trucks ran over your cow?" asks the new customer.

Sarala smiles. "All that is for rich people who live in tall buildings," she says. "The truck driver will say that it was my cow's fault to stand on the road. He is probably feeling terrible about hitting a cow. Why torture him some more?"

We all make clucking noises, borrowed from the rooster that is digging the earth nearby. (This is the rooster that wakes me—and my irate French neighbor—at 4:30 a.m. every morning. We both want to wring his strutting neck, furious as we are with his cocky sideways gaze, and dense, hot comb. But he belongs to the recycling shop next door to us. Wish as we might, we cannot recycle him to the next world.)

"The people in our area said that if we went and complained to the police, something would come of it," says Naidu. "But we decided not to pursue it. Who has the time to go and hang around the police?"

I nod, admiring how Naidu has turned his impotence with the police into a choice. There is a certain bravado in the way Naidu speaks that comes from years of having converted resigned acceptance into free will—at least in his mind. Instead of cursing how the poor are disenfranchised in the country (which he does sometimes), instead of complaining about how they don't have the clout to make headway with the city government (which he knows they don't), Naidu says that it was their "choice" to drop the matter. He has recast the situation into one that he chose to avoid. Is this how rationalization works?

"Cows and me don't set at all," says Naidu. "Because I married her," he nods at Sarala, "I am stuck in this profession." A hardship he has lamented before.

Set is a word I hear frequently among the people who energize and lubricate my life here in Bangalore. When I refer a driver or chauffeur to a neighbor for a job, he may report back after a week saying that the job "did not set," which means that it didn't work out. "Not setting" is a complaint, a failure, an impasse. It can mean that the employer was too strict or too stingy or merely that they didn't get along. It can mean that complex negotiations with a carpenter about teak wood versus fiberboard, and about whether he will throw in a chair with the table, are all on the verge of a breakdown for mysterious, unarticulated reasons that may have to do with strident tone, the price of raw teak, or the fact that the carpenter's assistant has just gotten engaged and is demanding higher wages. Any or all of these factors can cause negotiations not to set.

But it doesn't have to be a negotiation. For my milk lady, naming a cow is a crucial decision. She will give a tentative name to see if the name will set, if good things happen after the naming. If a name doesn't set, the cow will give less milk. Or get hit by a truck and die.

8

IF YOU DON'T LIKE THE MILK, CHANGE YOUR COW

IT IS A QUIET morning. The yellow school buses have left. The roads breathe some before the morning traffic begins, their din louder and more chaotic than New York. (When will I stop comparing these cities, and what is the point of doing so? It only makes me homesick and I am not even sure where "home" is anymore.)

The occasional garbage truck trundles down, rattling like a minor earthquake. Men on motorbikes drive on the quiet road, balancing precarious loads in between their legs—large bundles of vegetables, fruits, banana leaves, and greens that they will later sell to customers like me who have neither the time nor the inclination to go to City Market to buy weekly vegetables in bulk. Food carts, carrying life's necessities—buttermilk, tea, tobacco—get pushed down the road like convenience stores on wheels.

Sarala stands behind her large stainless-steel milk drum, smiling and nodding like a benevolent Buddha. Customers crowd around. Her drum is filled with frothy milk. Sarala holds her orange-colored, plastic sieve over her customers' containers and pours out the requested quantity of milk: one, two, or three liters. Picky customers wait for the milk that is being drawn at that moment. They prefer single-origin milk, straight from one cow's udder into their container. They like the smell and feel of just-expressed milk, still warm from the cow's body. The milk in Sarala's big steel drum is a blend—originating from three different cows. Most people don't mind the blend. They are in a hurry. They walk up, hand Sarala their milk coupons, stick out their stainless-steel buckets, collect the milk, and walk away.

I usually prefer single-origin milk. This morning I, too, am in a hurry. The plumber who has reneged four times has promised that he will show up to fix the leak in our bathroom.

"Mother-promise, Madam," he pronounced solemnly, when I phoned him last night. "God-promise."

"Don't say that," I admonished. "If you don't come tomorrow, your mother will die."

I didn't know then that his mother was already dead.

Selva squats nearby, milking Sarala's favorite cow, a black-nosed beauty that stamps often to shoo away flies. Sarala has names for each of her ten cows. This one is Chella Lakshmi, or "Sweetheart" Lakshmi—the cow that Malu and I attempted to milk—but most of us merely point at the bovines.

The street and sidewalk are not that different from those on the Upper West Side in Manhattan. Except that in place of bicycles chained to trees and posts, there are live cows waiting in line. Instead of grocery or milk trucks, there are cows. Instead of delivery boys, there is young Selva, squatting on the ground, milking a cow.

Hawk-eyed customers from the army campus watch Selva. Their stainless-steel milk cans, lined up beside each other, look like Indian ubersculptor Subodh Gupta's installations. Parakeets shriek overhead as they fly in streaks of green.

A woman wearing a purple hijab walks towards us. Her name is Mumtaz and she is one of the regulars. She tells Sarala that her son Ahmed doesn't like Chella Lakshmi's milk. She wants milk from her "usual cow," a dark-skinned beauty that stands a few yards away placidly chewing cucumber peels.

I stare at six-year-old Ahmed doubtfully. Clad in his blue-and-white school uniform, with neatly parted wet hair and soulful eyes, he seems too young to have a palate, let alone one that can differentiate between the milk of two cows. The lad stares back at me in the unblinking fashion of children.

"Can your son tell the difference?" I ask.

"Of course," Mumtaz says, with a toss of her purple hijab. "Can't you?" She points at the cow eating cucumber peels. "The dark cow's milk is more . . . how to say it . . . more stable, more gentle. It has less . . . intensity and settles well in the stomach. It's all the cucumber that she eats. It makes her milk more . . . "

"Alkaline?"

"If you want to call it that," Mumtaz says, nodding.

She takes me aside and quietly tells me to stay away from the milk of the far cow. "It's these Americans, you see. They have been importing mangoes and giving the mango peels to that cow. Who eats mangoes in November? The poor cow gorges on mango peels and its milk has become gassy, acidic. My son gets an upset stomach after drinking that one's milk."

It occurs to me that I am hearing a new solution to lactose intolerance: change your cow.

SARALA AND I ARE both South Indian. She can speak my language, Tamil, but I cannot speak her mother tongue Telugu. Most of her customers from the army complex are North Indians who speak Hindi and cannot speak either of our languages. This is why Indians are so good at picking up English: we have too many regional languages.

"That lady is too shrewd," Sarala tells me in Tamil after Mumtaz leaves with milk from her preferred cow. "She can line up all my cows and tell tiny-tiny differences in the milk with arrow-like precision."

Indians will rarely say "tiny" in the singular. It usually involves what my father, the English professor, calls "reduplication," or repeating the same or a similar, rhyming word. Indian languages are full of reduplication, as well as onomatopoeia. Perhaps we do this to make ourselves heard in a noisy land.

I do the same thing when my plumber arrives, two hours late.

"*Besh-besh*," I say. "Thank you for showing up."

Besh-besh is like saying, "Well, well." It means different things based on tone of voice. It can be a compliment, express sarcasm, or convey amazement.

"I was in another house, Madam. They were *noy-noy* [bugging me]."

"Okay, then. Don't stand around *masa-masa* [dithering like this]," I reply. "Come fast-fast and do some work."

"I would have sent my son," the plumber says, unpacking his tools. "But all he does is talk *loda-loda* [loudly]. He is such a waste. And fat, too."

"Don't worry," I say. "You will conduct his wedding *jaam-jaam*, [with pomp and circumstance]. Just watch. All your problems will be solved."

"Oh, don't talk about my wastrel son's marriage. My heart is racing *pada-pada* [pitter-patter] already," says the plumber, his head underneath my washbasin.

"Why do you worry? Let me make you some *chuda-chuda* [hot-hot] coffee and everything will be alright."

Besh-besh; chuda-chuda; gada-gada; mada-mada; pada-pada; masa-masa; loda-loda; ada-ada; chinna-chinna. These are the phrases I grew up with, as comforting to me as a mother's heartbeat. Bengali, the North Indian language of Nobel Prize–winning poet Rabindranath Tagore and of cult film director Satyajit Ray, is perhaps the queen of reduplication, with a whole host of phrases that are musical and emphatic: *phit-phat*, *ghup-ghap*, *tok-tok*, and other expressions made up of words that are said twice, and sometimes thrice for emphasis.

South Indian languages are not far behind. Some expressions, like the Tamilian "ada-ada" and "besh-besh," are just exclamations that change the meaning of the sentence depending on tone of voice. But reduplication isn't really about tone. It is used to give an expression some girth. *Tiny*, for instance, is a tiny word, so Indians will rarely say it in the singular. In the film *Monsoon Wedding*, there is a scene comparing a woman's breasts to mangoes and one speaker uses the term, *choti-choti aam* ("tiny-tiny mangoes").

Indians use reduplication to convey two contrary impulses: intensity and casualness. And Sarala's use of reduplication gives her speech an onomatopoeic cadence, both soothing and descriptive to the people who crowd around her every morning.

"Is it true, what Mumtaz said?" I ask one morning. "Do different cows have different types of milk?"

"Of course," says Sarala with her typical, breezy confidence. "Each breed of cow gives a different type of milk depending on its body type, temperament, what it has eaten, whether it is in heat. So many factors."

"What if I want the best cow's milk?" I ask.

"There is no best cow's milk," she says. "It is like a marriage. Will one man's wife be suitable as a spouse for another man?"

"Yes," I say. "Isn't that why marriages break up?"

Her face falls. I feel a pinch of regret for spoiling what she thought was a perfect example.

"But go on," I prod.

Sarala stares at me, as if trying to decide the best way to describe a complex concept to a moron.

According to Sarala, anything from nature, be it picking fruits, vegetables, or flowers, or foraging for mushrooms and herbs, isn't simply a matter of what we humans call "quality." It isn't only about the size of the fruit or how unblemished the vegetable looks. Those are considerations but there is also energy, resonance, destiny.

"Say you go to buy a puppy," she says. "There will be lots of puppies in the yard. Why do you choose the one you do? You may say that it is because the puppy is cute or beautiful. But it is a lot more than that. Maybe the puppy and you were friends in your past life. Maybe the puppy has been created to come into your home and teach you something—patience, courage, something. It is the same with milking."

"Even today, it happens like this in villages," says Sarala. "My aunt knows exactly which cow to choose for the day's milk for her family. Some of it is intuition. You choose a cow based on its mood, what it looks like, what the day feels like, what you feel like, whether someone in your family has a fever or cold, whether the planets are properly aligned. It is like Mumtaz said. During the exams, you want the milk of an active cow. When you are sick, you want buffalo's milk because it will put you to sleep. If there are four cows in your shed, you choose the one to milk for your family and give the remaining milk away. Today, it is all standardized. You don't know where your milk is coming from."

What Sarala says is music to my ears. Synchronicity. Serendipity. Destiny. Nebulous intangibles that speak to my soul and spirit. I gaze at the four cows that stand beside me under the trees. The idea of choosing a cow to suit a specific family's needs—for that day, moment, and space—is alluring.

"How do I learn this intuition for choosing milk?"

Sarala gazes at me. Something in the sincerity of my question and demeanor suggests to her that I am serious. "Go see my brother," she says simply.

SARALA'S "BROTHER" ISN'T REALLY her brother, not in the Western sense of the term, anyhow. He is her distant relative, male, and older than she is, so she calls him "Anna" ("elder brother"). The Indian mind seeks relationships over transactions; it values connection more than opportunities. Friends become family. Why call someone a friend when she can be your older brother or sister?

Sarala's brother is a farmer in Dinnur village just outside of Bangalore. One morning, I drive there to learn about cows and intuition and choosing milk. The meeting point is vague.

"My brother will be standing opposite Ideal Store, with his fruit-cart. This time of year, he will be selling watermelons and pineapples," says Sarala.

Bordered by lily ponds and mango orchards, the picturesque village is full of compact homes. Each home has a courtyard with cows. Sarala's brother is exactly where she said he would be. On the single country lane is a solitary shop called Ideal Store. Opposite is a turbaned fruit seller. He squints at me in the sunlight. I introduce myself in fluent Tamil as Sarala's friend. Nambi breaks out into a broad smile and offers me some tender coconut water. I feel bad that I am taking freebies from a fruit seller. I offer to buy one of his watermelons.

"Why must you buy? You are Sarala's friend. Here." In quick order, he splits open a watermelon and cuts it into glistening pink cubes. Both of us chew watermelon cubes, spit out the seeds, and talk desultorily. Nambi sees a cut on my arm and suggests that I use a poultice made of raw onions and garlic on the wound.

"With the price of onions and garlic being what they are, I'd rather go to an English doctor [allopathic doctor]," I reply.

Commiserating over the price of vegetables is, along with

bargaining, a great Indian pastime. It is a way to connect instantly. Nambi nods heartily. He and I complain companionably about how we have stopped making onion chutneys and pilafs because the price of onions is so high.

"Thankfully, milk isn't so expensive," I say.

This is the opening Nambi is waiting for. He tells me about "desi" cows and the virtues of their milk. "What does 'desi' mean?" he asks, and waits for my answer, as a teacher would.

"Native," I say.

Nambi nods. "Desi means 'native, local.' A cow that has been bred in the region for generations, for centuries, so that its skin, hooves, eyes, and most importantly, milk quality is adapted to the environment."

Nambi isn't concerned with storied North Indian breeds like the Gir of Gujarat, Rathi of Rajasthan, and Sahiwal of Punjab—named after the regions where they are bred. He is interested in local South Indian breeds. Like Sarala, he comes from a village in Tamil Nadu that is home to ancient Tamil breeds like Kangeyam, Bargur, Pulikulam and Umblachery. The farmers right across the border in Karnataka raise Hallikar, Amrit Mahal, Malnad Gidda, and other cows.

We walk through tiny lanes, surrounded by lily ponds. Jewel beetles shining neon and blue sit somnolently on leaves. Blue and brown butterflies flutter about. Dragonflies buzz. We walk by a large grazing pasture with cows lying under the trees.

"That is a *vellamaram* tree," says Nambi. "Cows like eating its seeds but it comes out with the dung." He points out the different grasses that cattle feed on. There is *kolukattai* grass (*Cenchrus ciliaris*). It can retain moisture and disperse its seeds widely. There are thirty types of grasses that cows like to eat, he says, each with an evocative local name. There is *nandu pul* (crabgrass); *kudai pul* (purpletop Rhodes grass), which has an umbrella-shaped top; *ottam pul* (bristle grass); *vennam pul*, which means "white grass"; *kurutu pul* ("swollen windmill grass"); *chola pul*, which means "corn grass"; *arugam pul* (Bermuda grass); and a variety of creepers and shrubs.

"This one here cures cancer, they say. But we use it for sugar [diabetes]," says Nambi, pointing at a creeper called *nathai choori* (*Borreria hispida*).

When I look it up later, I discover papers in Sciencedirect.com corroborating its cancer-fighting properties. The other creepers that cows favor have beautiful tiny flowers: *hadupudukanam* (*Rhynchosia rufescens*) with its yellow flowers; *cheppunerunji* (*Indigofera enneaphylla*) with its plump, pink flowers; and *savarikodi* (*Merremia tridentata*), or arrow-leaf morning glory. Traditional ayurveda therapies use these plants to improve renal function and alleviate urinary-system diseases.

Ayurveda views milk as a cure-all. Short of finding you a spouse, milk, it seems, can achieve a lot, particularly in the personal health area. The *Rig Veda* extols milk as an ambrosia—one that confers eternal youth. Vasishta, a legendary sage, drank milk from the cow Nandini and remained youthful for ten thousand years. Did the ancients imbue milk with all these qualities because they hadn't discovered, say, beer and wine?

In the *Charaka Samhita*, one of the two foundational ayurvedic texts, milk is one of nine products that can be consumed throughout your life, the others being rice, pulses, rock salt, fruits, barley, rain water, ghee, and honey. Sadly, samosas, pizza, and tiramisu, my three favorite foods, don't make the cut in terms of daily diet.

Ayurvedic texts list a mind-boggling array of benefits that milk offers. "Milk is generally sweet, unctuous, coolant, lactogenic, refreshing, and nourishing," one of the texts begins. So far so good. But another text also attributes the following properties to milk: "aphrodisiac, useful for intelligence, strength-giving, useful for mental faculties, invigorating, fatigue-dispelling, a reliever of dyspnea and bronchitis."

Is milk an aphrodisiac? Is this why newlywed Indian couples are offered a glass of hot milk spiked with cardamom and saffron before they head to the honeymoon suite to spend their first night together? Because hot milk promotes a romp in the proverbial hay?

Dairy farmers like Sarala and Nambi believe that linking milk to goodness is only part of the story. The real reason that milk is so good is because it comes from the cow.

"Just think about it," says Nambi. "A cow eats all these medicinal herbs and grasses and gives us all these wonderful things through its milk. That is the magic of cow's milk. That is why we worship this animal."

9

LAND OF A MILLION COWS

INDIA HAS ROUGHLY 300 million bovines, the most of any country in the world. Nambi's municipality has a fair sample of these animals. Over the next hour, we drive through tiny lanes in search of storied breeds. Some homes are twenty minutes away, some in the next lane. All are occupied by dairy farmers.

Nambi opens the gate of one home. Inside stands a stunning cow with two horns rising straight up. It is a Bargur cow: red with white patches. Like all *Bos indicus* cows, it has a distinctive hump on its back. As soon as we walk in, the cow stamps and snorts. I revise my opinion about cows as meek and passive. This one looks ready to gore us—sizing us up through the side of its eyes.

"Hey, hey," Nambi shouts, tightening the cow's rope.

Hearing the noise, the owner of the cow ambles out of his home, suppressing a yawn. He is dressed in a turban and dhoti, just like Nambi.

"This is the lady I was telling you about," says Nambi. "The journalist. She is writing about cows and wants to interview us."

I smile at the spin Sarala has put on this meeting. I consider pulling out my notebook and pen, just to look official, but the cow is taking all their attention. They are sweet-shouting at her, trying to get her to calm down. She isn't used to strangers, says the owner apologetically. Not like the city cows that can stand in the middle of a street without getting ruffled. I swallow as I remember the dead cow on the street. Seems like Sarala hasn't told Nambi about the mishap.

After the cow calms down, the owner offers us some—what else—milk. His wife brings out a stainless-steel tumbler filled to the brim with plain white milk. Is it safe? Is it sanitary, I think to myself?

Nambi glances at my face. "Don't worry. The milk has been boiled. What's more, it has medicinal value. No diabetes or blood pressure if you drink this."

With such a stirring recommendation, I feel compelled to taste the hot milk. The two men are looking at me expectantly.

"Do you taste it?" they ask.

"What?"

"The herbs and grass that she has eaten?"

I shake my head.

"She is not able to taste the difference because we boiled the milk," says the owner regretfully. "To truly enjoy milk, you have to taste it straight from the udder. Raw. Fresh."

I down the contents of the glass before they take the idea any further.

"Delicious," I say.

"What does it taste of?" asks the owner of the cow.

"Milk? Herbs? Hay?" I venture.

They nod approvingly.

The milk tasting continues. In another village is a Kangeyam cow, a sturdy draft animal that is native to these parts. The same routine happens. Nambi hands me some boiled milk.

"We can sell a Kangeyam cow's milk for double the price of normal milk," says Nambi. "People come long distances to buy this milk."

Then comes an Umblachery. By the fifth cow, I can tell the difference. Or at least I have identified some parameters by which I can tell the difference. I hate to sound like a pretentious wine snob, but it has to do with the scent of the earth, the hints of hay, the herbaceous notes, and the heaviness or lightness of texture. Also, how I feel after drinking each cow's milk.

"Does the personality of the milkman matter?" I ask.

They stare at me.

"You know, just as the quality of the food has to do with the mood and temperament of the chef," I explain.

Oh sure, they say. But I know that they aren't buying my theory.

The life of a dairy farmer is brutal. They don't have the time or energy for niceties. I am being naïve. And of course thinking that tasty food comes from a happy chef is a view that will be overturned by anyone who has entered a restaurant kitchen. Similarly, dairy farmers mostly scold, shout, slap, and prod their cows. I have never seen a milkman who sings to a cow. They may feel affection for it but that gets lost in the busyness of the milking cycle. Just like you wouldn't know I love my kids if you came to our home at 6:30 a.m. and listened to me yelling and threatening them to get ready for school.

Milk from a Malnad Gidda is lighter than that of a Hallikar. A Malnad cow is used to a rainy monsoon climate, says Nambi. The people it serves are prone to monsoon-induced mucus—coughs and colds. As a result, its milk has evolved to be less mucus-giving, more medicinal with antibodies against the flu and cold season. The Hallikar prefers calcium-rich grasses. Drinking just a shot of Hallikar milk is enough to give you enough strength for a bullfight. Drinking milk from these cows, says Nambi, is the way to live, because such milk gives not just nutrients but also antibodies that prevent and improve health.

"You will never get a cold if you drink a desi cow's milk," he says.

This is when I get excited. In Bangalore, a number of residents are allergic to parthenium (feverfew); for them the plant causes runny nose, sneezing, and asthma. Perhaps local breeds ate parthenium-type plants, and as a result their milk might help people develop a resistance to the allergens in the environment? Nambi doesn't understand my long-winded explanation but nods anyway.

INDIA'S NATIONAL BUREAU OF Animal Genetic Resources lists forty indigenous breeds of cattle, all belonging to the *Bos indicus* species. The actual number is more like sixty-five, which, activists say, is down from the 110 to 130 native breeds that India used to have. They range from the Vechur, the size of a golden retriever; to the mighty Brahman that has now been exported to and is popular in Brazil; to the aristocratic Amrit Mahal cow that delivers what farmers believe is the nectar of immortality, from all orifices of the body; to the Red Sindhi cow, with its lovely hanging dewlaps and high hump on its back; to the Gir, which has half-moon-shaped horns that add to its inquiring gaze; to the Tharparkar, which can cross deserts on only a single drink of water; to the Punjabi Sahiwal that delivers the highest quantity of milk.

The problem is that Indian cows have been crossbred with foreign Holstein-Friesian and Jersey breeds to the point where the indigenous Indian cow may become extinct. An Indo-Canadian environmental protection NGO called Ankush lists twenty-seven Indian breeds that are already extinct. These breeds, distinct and specific to their regions, evolved over millennia. Umblachery cows have shorter legs than the Kangeyam, for instance, which makes it easier for them to walk around the swampy, marshy, water-fed regions of the river delta where they live. The hilly-region cows such as the Malai Maadu and the Malnad Gidda are as agile as goats over mountainous terrain. The quality of their milk is different, too.

Holstein-Friesian (HF) is the most common breed among dairy farmers in Bangalore. These are the cows that Sarala owns and milks. Are native Indian cows all that different from these high-yielding hybrids? As it turns out, they are. Some ten thousand years ago, a genetic mutation occurred amongst cattle, causing the beta casein (or protein) in their milk to convert from what is called "A2" to "A1" milk.

All the Indian breeds deliver the premutation A2-type milk. So do camels, sheep, goats, donkey, buffaloes, and yaks. So do Jersey cows—the indigenous Western hemisphere breed.

Now here is the thing: some research has shown that the premutational, ancient A2 milk is better than A1 milk, in terms of health benefits. A big proponent of this theory is Keith Woodford, a professor in New Zealand and author of *Devil in the Milk: Illness, Health, and the Politics of A1 and A2 Milk* (with the rather specific subtitle, lest you had doubts about its content or point of view). In his book, Woodford suggests that the type of milk we consume these days might well be the cause of much of the health ailments that we endure.

Studies link A1 milk, which most of us consume these days, to irritable bowel syndrome, diarrhea, bloating, arteriosclerosis, type 1 diabetes, and even autism and schizophrenia. A study titled, "Polymorphism of Bovine Beta-casein and Its Potential Effect on Human Health," listed in PubMed, states that "neurological disorders, such as autism and schizophrenia, seem to be associated with milk consumption and a higher level of BCM-7," which is found in A1 milk.

Proponents of A2 believe that milk from indigenous breeds like Guernsey and Jersey and the *Bos indicus* species is better than milk from hybrid breeds such as Holstein-Friesian. In the US, for instance, a company called a2 Milk sells what it calls "the original milk that feels better" at The Fresh Market and other specialty stores. In India, though, milk from *Bos indicus* cows is still the "alternative" milk.

"I want to buy milk from a desi cow, not a crossbreed," I say.

Nambi nods and agrees. "We all know that milk from desi breeds is better," he says. "The problem is that they only give a few liters: enough for a family but not for a livelihood. Only Hare Krishna ashrams sell this type of milk."

His family owned an Amrit Mahal, a fabled gray breed that was developed in the eighteenth century by Tipu Sultan. The cow's milk was like nectar, he says, even though it wasn't a great milker. They had to send it out to pasture, a euphemism for saying that it died of old age. "It ate some specific grasses that compressed her kidneys and slowly called it a day," says Nambi. "What an amazing animal it was. Could outrun a horse. Now we are stuck with these half-breeds."

Detractors link the demise of the desi cow to India's "white revolution." In 1970, India's National Dairy Development Board (NDDB) launched Operation Flood. It created a grid linking small dairy farmers to consumers. And what a flood that created! India surpassed the United States in 1998 as the world's largest producer of milk. Focusing on milk output, however, was a death knell to the low-yielding native cows.

Had we stuck to local cows, perhaps so many Indians would not be diabetic. That is the message that organizations such as the Desi Cows for Better India Trust want to promote. Sarala also believes that the milk from native cows is special. The problem is that they give less milk than her HF cows. "If I could charge more per liter for native cow's milk, my entire herd would be Hallikars or Amrit Mahal cows," she says.

"Indians should market cow's milk like the French market cheese," says Sajal Kulkarni, a researcher with BAIF Development Research Foundation in Pune. "We have to create niche, high-end markets like in France and Italy. We need to charge a higher rate for local indigenous cow's milk that is suited to the Indian climate and region."

Should we feel bad that these specialized breeds are going extinct? Or shrug our shoulders and call it evolution and economics?

10

THE SCATOLOGICAL REMNANTS
OF A COW

ONE DAY, SOMETHING WEIRD happens. Selva is milking the cows as usual. When he is done with one cow, he carries over the steel bucket full of milk. We all stretch our cans out—like kids collecting candy.

One of Sarala's regulars, a tall, thin man with cropped army hair, always carries an empty Coke bottle with him. That day, I find out why. As we converge around the milk can, one of the cows starts urinating. The army man jumps out of our circle, races to the cow, and holds out the Coke bottle so that the urine can be collected in it.

When cows let off, it is like a fire hose that has burst open. It doesn't dribble; it's more like a waterfall. The army man tries to angle his plastic bottle so that the urine won't touch his fingers—to no avail. By the time the cow is done, the bottle is almost full. He walks back to us with a slight smile. My daughters would call it "the grossest thing" that they have ever seen, but everyone around nods approvingly.

"What does he do with the urine?" I ask Sarala after the crowd has dispersed.

"I'm not sure," she replies. "You can put it on your plants as a fertilizer; you can mix it with herbs and take it like a tea. Cow urine is an amazing substance. Practically a cure-all."

I don't believe her. I think she is making it up, exaggerating the benefits of cows as usual.

Over the next several days, I befriend the army man and ask him what he does with the cow urine.

"I drink it," he replies gravely.

How do you respond when someone tells you this—that they drink cow urine? You can either plunge in with more questions or retreat in a cloud of apologies. I choose the former. Does he just drink the urine straight up, like a shot of, say, tequila? Or does he dilute it like green tea? Does he also mix it with food, sprinkling it over oatmeal porridge, like people do with flaxseeds on their salad?

You cannot drink cow urine straight up, he says, looking me in the eye. "It is too much medicinal. I put it in a terra-cotta pot, keep it in a dark, cool place for several days, and allow the sediments to settle. After a week, the clean, clear liquid comes to the top. It is like distillation. Then I scoop out the top part and drink it. Just a teaspoon a day will do."

You know how it is when something bizarre enters your world-view and you start to see it everywhere? That is how it is with cow urine for me.

One evening, as I run on the treadmill in the gym next door, I watch Sarala's husband herd his cows for the dusk milking. One of his cows urinates as she walks. Sure enough, out springs a man from within a mechanic shop. He chases the cow as she walks, situating a green Sprite bottle to catch the urine. The cow tries to shoo him off by waving her tail from side to side, but the man is undeterred. He fills his bottle and leaves. Does he pour the cow urine on the cars that have come for repair? Is it for lubricating stuck wheels?

"You should charge people for the urine," I tell Sarala flippantly one day. She stares at me. I realize that she takes my remark seriously.

"You know, since my family has kept cows for generations, I have started thinking like a cow," she says. "How does a cow think?"

Is she testing me? I blink. I have no idea. I can't figure out what she wants me to say. How does a cow think? Does it think of milk? That seems most obvious.

Thankfully, she puts me out of my misery.

"How does a cow think?" she asks. This time, I know it is a rhetorical question. "A cow thinks generously, right? Like she is the mother of humanity," Sarala answers herself.

I nod even though I don't agree that a cow has such a macro view on life. It probably thinks about hay and grass and its next meal, not about the milk of human kindness or consumption.

"A cow is the most generous animal in the whole world," Sarala continues. "Every part of her does good for humans. Even her urine. How can I charge you for cow urine when I take care of animals of this caliber, of this level of generosity?"

I don't remind her that she has no problem charging for the animal's milk. What is the difference?

At a party, I recount my witnessing of people catching cow's urine. However, I don't get the chuckles I am hoping for. I don't even get the winking "isn't India crazy?" looks that usually accompany my "only in India" tales. One of my friends, a high-level executive at Cisco Systems who has just returned from Berlin, tells me that he is giving his mother cow urine as treatment. She has stage IV ovarian cancer, he says.

"The doctors gave her three months to live. She didn't want to undergo chemotherapy. So we gave her these herbal pills made from cow urine. She has been cancer-free for three years now," he says.

I discover that an aunt of mine has been bathing in cow urine for years. Not the unadulterated stuff, but she mixes a small cup of urine into a bucket of water and pours it over her body—before a final shower rinse with plain hot water, thankfully. Is this why her skin is so soft and wrinkle-free?

The trick is in sourcing the cow urine, everyone says. You have to get it from free-range, Indian cows that know which grass to eat according to season and time of day. If you can get the first urine of the day from a cow that hasn't calved, even better.

It turns out that there are a few organizations in India that sell distilled cow urine. One is in Bangalore. And so it comes to be that I stand outside a clinic with a billboard that reads: "Dr. Jain's Ayurvedic and Cow Urine Therapy."

"For Chronic Diseases: Cancer, HIV, Tuberculosis, Piles, Asthma, Sugar, Joint Aches, etc.," the next line breezily proclaims.

The clinic in Bangalore is an outpost of the mother ship in Indore, where some thirty-five hundred indigenous cows are raised
for their products. The urine of black cows is given for cancer,
white cows for skin diseases, and red cows for gynecological problems. Adjacent to the multi-acre farm is a center where the cow
urine is distilled and mixed with ayurvedic herbs. The clinic con-
ducts health camps in which hundreds of people line up to drink
a shot glass full of cow urine as a protective measure.

"Look at it this way," says the man who runs Dr. Jain's Bangalore
franchise. "There are certain indigenous herbs that treat certain
diseases, but by the time we pick, preserve, package, and distribute
these herbs, they have lost their potency. Immersing the herbs in
cow urine not only protects them from degradation but also increases their potency."

Over the next hour, he explains to me why cow urine is so important medically. It has antibacterial, antioxidant, anticancer, and
antifungal properties. It enhances the immune system and counteracts the toxic effects of cancer drugs. Cow urine is an elixir of
health, and a strengthener of the heart, intelligence, and long life. It
cleanses the blood and balances the three *doshas* (imbalances due to
excess bile/heat, excess mucus, and excess air that cause bloating).
It cures heart diseases and counteracts the effect of poison. Wow!

Urine from foreign or hybrid HF cows won't do, he says. (I
make a mental note not to mention this to the people collecting
urine from Sarala's HF cows.) Only the *Bos indicus* species has the
surya-ketu nadi—a type of nerve channel in the raised hump of
the Indian cow. This channel attracts and absorbs the health benefits from the sun's rays and repels all its evil radiation. This is why
the products of Indian cows are so curative. Indian cows have that

special meridian that absorbs good vibrations from the sun, sky, stars, planets, and mother earth.

It's true that at first I laughed at drinking cow urine, but feed me a good story and I can believe anything. I am into alternative practices. Over the course of my long if totally unremarkable career as a wannabe healer, I have studied pulse diagnosis, salt therapy, Rolfing, the Feldenkrais Method, and everything in between. If you tell me, as one Japanese sensei did, that whirling like a dervish will center and connect you to the universal energy floating around, I will believe you. For a month, I woke up and whirled around in my kitchen while my coffee brewed. I listened to what the universe said, but couldn't fathom it. In New York I occasionally opened my trusty *I Ching* notebook to figure out if my journalism professor would be in a good mood that day and not chew me out for being late to class. I tried cowrie divination methods in Taos, where I worked as a camp counselor during my senior year in college.

When the cow urine doctor tells me that Indian cows have a special meridian that links them to the sun and planets, it is music to my ears. Then he goes into a long explanation about the influence of planets on our life, and about how a lot of what happens to us is predestined. He says there is a way we can increase "synchronicity," or good coincidences. "Living in the groove," he calls it. Aligned with the earth and other species. Cow urine is a pathway to synchronicity, he says. "Drink it for a month and you will start thinking and looking like a twenty-year-old," he says.

I have heard Deepak Chopra talk about synchronicity and have been trying to game it ever since—through astronomy, astrology, whirling, whatever. Cow urine is now on my list.

"I have hypothyroidism," I tell the doctor. "Will cow urine help me cure that?"

He shakes his head. "Why don't you take Thyronorm—thyroxine sodium—tablets? One a day and it will balance out your thyroid."

I am both impressed and disappointed. Had he been a quack doctor, it would have been easy for him to say yes, that cow urine would cure my hypothyroidism. I am trying so many alternative measures anyway—performing yogic headstands, drinking tulsi (holy basil) tea, massaging my thyroid, and practicing distance Reiki healing. Had my TSH levels come back to normal, the doctor could have claimed that cow urine was the cause. Instead he prescribes Thyronorm, which I am taking anyway. While I respect his honesty, part of me wanted to believe that cow urine really is a panacea.

As he speaks, a steady stream of people comes in and collects bottles of cow urine distillate—for themselves, for parents, for wives. Many have cancer. The doctor gives me the names and phone numbers of eight patients he has treated and cured—all using cow urine. I call them.

One woman's name is Katherine, and she had been given up for dead at a hospital. "The doctors called me a body, not a person. Can you believe it?" she asks, clearly outraged. "Told my kids to come and take the body." Her children, too, had given up hope. Funeral arrangements had been made. As a last resort, Katherine's brother, who had heard about cow urine, gave her a teaspoon the night they brought her home. When she opened her eyes the next morning, they gave her more cow urine—a teaspoon twice a day for about a week. "This was six years ago," says Katherine. "I am still alive."

Another man is a tailor whose wife had cancer. She, too, was cured because of cow urine therapy, he says. The third is a lady from the United States who gave cow urine to her Indian father-in-law. "He had been bedridden for years. After seven months of this treatment, he could walk to the post office and back," she says.

My mother-in-law hears me speaking on the phone to the cow-urine-therapy patients. Maybe this will cure my joint aches, too, she says. She struggles with sciatica and depends on giant bottles of Move Free that her daughter, a pediatrician in the United States, buys for her from Costco.

So one morning my mother-in-law and I go to the clinic and purchase some pills and powders that will help her joint aches. The cow urine doctor tells her to take one packet a day.

Like me, my mother-in-law is naturally inclined towards alternative medicine. She distrusts allopathic drugs and prefers to go the natural route. When the doctor gives her packets of powders, she asks what they contain.

"Cow dung," he says. "Dried cow dung along with other ayurvedic herbs."

She doesn't blink. "Somehow the South Indian mind doesn't think of cow dung as dirty," she tells me later. "We have grown up around cow dung."

I nod. It isn't really true. My husband and others in my family are South Indian, but they don't necessarily warm to cow urine, and I highly doubt cow dung will go over well either. I think it has more to do with my mother-in-law's personality and her openness.

The man throws in a free bottle of cow urine for me to try.

I don't plan to tell the rest of my family but I do happen to mention at dinner that the Sanskrit term for cow urine is *go-mutra*. My children burst out laughing.

"What's so funny?" I ask. "Anything beginning with a *go* has to do with the cow in India. Places like Goa, Godavari, Gomukh, Gokarna are linked to the cow as are human names like Gopal, Govind, and Gokul—"

"And go-mutra," they chorus, giggling.

That night, I stare at the small bottle of cow urine—go-mutra—wondering whether to sample it.

What will my husband say? What will my sister-in-law say? I know the answers. They will be horrified. They will think I am mad. Where are the randomized, double-blind clinical trials, they will ask.

Ram and his only sister, Lakshmi (a physician), have rational, scientific bents of mind. Lakshmi's husband, Krishnan, is an internist. Amazing doctors, both—healers in the true spirit of the word. They have a thriving private practice in Fort Myers, Florida. We depend on them for all of our medical needs. So does an ever-expanding circle of people.

Every time they visit us in Bangalore, they are literally stopped on the street with medical questions. Our building doorman has a question about why his wife isn't conceiving. He shows all of his wife's blood reports to Krishnan, who scans and sends them to his golf buddy, a gynecologist. The gynecologist is in the midst of a golf vacation when the tattered scanned copies arrive. But he responds, as doctors do for colleagues, and Krishnan prescribes medication for the doorman's wife.

Word gets around. The building plumber approaches my sister-in-law. His daughter has a kidney stone, or so he thinks. She isn't eating enough. And so it goes, every single time. Housekeepers, gardeners, security guards, and the odd plumber approach them for free medical advice, which they give patiently and generously.

AFTER OUR MEETING WITH the cow-urine doctor, my mother-in-law and I bring the cow-urine bottle and the powder that he gives us into the house. My mother-in-law lines up the cow-dung powder beside her Tylenol and Move Free bottles.

I finally open the cow-urine bottle after a particularly heavy lunch.

"Take one teaspoon twice a day," reads the label.

I hold my nose and down a small amount straight to the back of my mouth and swallow It tastes spicy, hot, and potent, like ammonia. Clears my sinuses right out. I feel like puking but control it. I think about honey, chocolate, and samosas. I try to distract my mind till the nausea passes. And then I brush my teeth.

As for my mother-in-law, the cow powder eases her pain, she says. After just three days of taking the medication.

Again, I can hear Ram's voice in my head. Are you sure these are really cow urine pills? he will ask. What if they are chemicals masked as cow urine medication? And even if it is authentic cow urine, what if there are side effects, just like with Western medications? Or what if all this improvement is a placebo effect?

This is the paradox of alternative medicine, isn't it? You have to believe in it in order to enjoy its benefits. My mother-in-law and I certainly are true, if covert, believers in these cow byproducts. But maybe we are just drawn to anything natural. If you tell us that eating dirt will help improve health, we will happily try it. At least you know what you are eating, instead of with those pills with unpronounceable names.

How did ancient humans learn that cow urine had a beneficial effect? Did some early *Homo sapiens* have excruciating joint pain? After trying out all the usual shoots, leaves, and roots that the clan ate to alleviate pain, did he or she hit upon the animal kingdom? "Maybe I'll try some cow urine?" he may have thought. Or perhaps some monks noticed the goats prancing around all night after eating coffee berries and decided to eat the same in order to study all night. Maybe ancient man noticed that the grass grew verdantly on the spots where the cows urinated. "Heck, this stuff is causing vegetation to grow more lush. Maybe it will improve the health of humans, too."

How did they test the effects of the urine of different animals? Did everyone in the nomadic tribe try the urine of cows and realize that it cleared out the sinuses? "Okay, let us now try horse urine and see what it does." A thousand people tried horse urine. Isn't this a clinical trial, albeit in the time before patents were filed?

Actually, the cow-urine clinic in Indore has filed two US patents (patent numbers 6410059 and 6896907) for drugs based on cow-urine distillates. But I don't need any of this scientific-sounding language or the numbers of patents in order to imbibe the stuff. Cow urine, for me, is like weed or acid or any of those other drugs that I definitely did not try while I was an art student in Massachusetts. It is like taking your first shot of vodka unbeknownst to your parents, like jumping through the window for a night out with your boyfriend while your folks assumed you were fast asleep. Cow urine has that whiff of danger and transgression—a substance, an action, that would be roundly condemned by the "adults" in our family.

Even at my age, maybe that's where its true attraction lies. When I finally tell my brother that I have tried cow urine, he wrinkles his face and practically disowns me. Then he suggests I must have suffered a genetic mutation.

A week later, I meet an acquaintance on the street. "You look fabulous," she says. "What have you done to yourself?"

11

COW MANURE FOR THE GARDEN

Our garden is dying from the heat. Our building complex has flowering shrubs, birds of paradise, a smallish lawn, and a few trees. The gardening committee—of which I am a member—fields suggestions. A neighbor proposes that we grow Indian hemp. All the garden waste—leaves, twigs, fallen flowers—will get easily broken down into compost for the garden. Another resident recommends cow manure. It is the oldest form of fertilizer, she says. An ashram nearby makes organic manure from cow dung. Why can't we duplicate their technique? I suggest a middle ground and offer to buy cow manure from a known source. It isn't Sarala I am thinking of. Rather, it is the mother ship of native cow excrement located an hour outside Bangalore. The place bills itself as the largest shelter for indigenous cows. Off I go.

I had expected a few cows and even fewer keepers. There are about a thousand people fussing over four hundred cows. The cows are sanguine and beautiful, with raised humps and sleek coats. A family clad in finery stands before a majestic Hallikar cow, feeding it bananas, bending with folded hands to get its blessings and showering it with pink hibiscus flowers.

"It is *amavasya* [new moon day]. Lots of businesspeople shut down their businesses and come here on this day to venerate the cow. Especially Jains. It is part of their religion," says B. J. Sharma, who founded the cow shelter upon the advice and instruction of his spiritual guru. India has many such cults.

Sharma tells me he was a diabetic for thirty-five years. For the last ten years, every morning and evening, he has been taking two teaspoons of cow urine mixed with an equal amount of water. His blood sugar has stabilized and he has become more active, he says.

A man brings over a stainless-steel tumbler of buttermilk, distributed free of cost to all visitors. "It is made from desi cow's milk. Very good for health," says Sharma. We down the liquid in one gulp. Cool and salty, it is delicious for a hot day. Reminds me of the Friendship brand of buttermilk that we used to buy at Fairway, Publix, and pretty much wherever we lived or traveled in the United States.

Urine collection is done manually, says Sharma. Five to ten men wake up at dawn with buckets. They go to the various cow pens and wake up the cows. They have to be fast. The minute one cow wakes and stands up, so do the others. It is like a relay race, or the falling of dominos. Except in reverse. A stack of cows stands up. Immediately after rising, the bovines do their business.

"Otherwise, you tickle their bottom and the urine comes out," says one of the keepers. "You have to run from cow to cow and catch its urine."

The urine is distilled in offsite plants and sold at the shelter. I buy a couple of bottles, as well as some cow dung, and go home.

A month later, our garden is thriving. The gardener swears that it is the cow dung that I have bought from the ashram. It is an elixir of life, he says, and then explains that out in the fields a cow knows exactly which part of the pasture needs nutrients. She only urinates and poops in those areas, says our gardener.

"What if she urgently needs to go?" I ask.

Even though my natural instinct is to lap up—literally and figuratively—pretty much every alternative theory that I encounter, this feels too far out. Plus, paradoxically, my other instinct is to be skeptical, just like Ram. Sounding much like my husband, the voice of reason, I argue with the gardener.

"I can't believe that the cow gets the urge to go and then searches for the exact spot where there is dying grass and then goes and poops on top of it," I say as we walk amidst fragrant jasmine creepers.

"Isn't there a lag time between when you get the urge to go and when you actually go?" asks the gardener in return. "When a cow is grazing in the pastures, it is not as if she needs to search for a bathroom. She just ambles to the spot where the ground needs nutrients, stands there and poops."

Our gardener repeats the same information I learned at Dr. Jain's Ayurvedic and Cow Urine Therapy about the humps on native cows. This time, though, it's cow dung that absorbs beneficial radiation from the sun and spreads positive energy. Like most stories about this animal, this statement is hard to prove or disprove, but these beliefs are widespread in India. For instance, one blog reports: "Many people, probably a million, died in the Bhopal gas tragedy but there was a township there where all the people were healthy, the reason being each and every house of the township was smeared with cow dung slurry and there were an innumerable number of tulsi plants growing. In ancient times people used to wash their feet and step on the doorstep smeared with cow-dung slurry before entering the house, which would kill all the germs, and the house remained free of pathogens."

Using this logic, Chernobyl should have imported cow dung after the blast.

Place a dried piece of cow dung inside your microwave when you defrost your food, says an acquaintance. It will absorb the harmful microwave radiation.

But won't it impart a bad smell, I ask?

Cow manure has no bad smell, she replies.

And so it goes, on and on with the cow dung and its uses.

Pretty soon, the manure that I bought at the ashram runs out. I approach Sarala yet again. When we first met, I had assumed that she would be the one making all the requests and I would be the one saying no. It isn't quite working out that way.

"Sarala, I need cow dung," I say without preamble.

"What kind of cow dung? Foreign breeds or native breeds?" she asks.

"Native cows," I say immediately.

A few days later, Sarala brings a blue bucket filled with cow dung. When that runs out, we relax our rules and decide to admit the cow dung of any cow into our manure pit. We buy a special, plastic drum for this purpose and hover around the cows when they come near our building. One day, I notice a plastic bag that comes out with the cow dung.

"You see what I told you," says Sarala triumphantly when I point it out. "These cows are very discriminating. Even when they nose around garbage, they know what to eat."

"Well, this cow ate plastic," I reply.

"Yes, but it took out the plastic through its dung, didn't it? It didn't retain the plastic in its belly."

"I saw a film in which there was a ton of plastic inside each cow," I say.

Sarala shakes her head. "If I keep a plate full of the choicest chicken or fish in front of you, will you eat it?"

"No," I reply.

"The cow's nose and mouth is ten times more sensitive than a human's. You think it is going to eat bones and plastic?"

Over the next few days, Sarala brings us more dung and we collect our own. After that, it is a simple matter of following the recipe. The end product is called *panchagavya*:

5 kilograms cow dung
5 liters cow urine
5 liters water
2 liters yogurt
2 liters cow's milk
500 milliliters ghee
1 kilogram black jaggery or molasses
Tender coconut water from two coconuts
5 bananas with peels

Mix all the above ingredients. Stir occasionally for three weeks. Then, it is ready to use.

There is an edible version of panchagavya, which I haven't tasted. I doubt that I could. But I don't dismiss it, either.

Perhaps ancient Indians were on to something. Or perhaps they found uses for whatever shit they had—literally. Rural Indians use dung to this day. Farmers plant seeds inside cow dung, as they consider it a seed protector and fertilizer. Dried cow dung is used as kindle in fires, burned as fuel for cooking, and applied as a mosquito repellent. It is thrown into ponds to balance pH. According to ayurveda, cow dung can be mixed into poultices and decoctions for malaria, snakebite, burns, and itching. It is coated on the walls and floors of mud houses to strengthen their construction; the adobe houses of New Mexico similarly.

But the most common use of cow dung is that of a purifier—weird and paradoxical, I know, but the practice is so widespread in India, both in the past and in rural areas today, that I've got to believe there is some truth in it. The dung is considered to have antibacterial and fungicidal properties. During the winter months rural (and even urban) households adorn their courtyards by sprinkling water diluted with dung on them, drawing beautiful *kolam* designs across the courtyard floors, and placing in the center a mound of cow dung topped with a yellow pumpkin flower. The brightness of the yellow flower contrasts nicely with the olive-green cow dung below it. Naturopath Dr. Sakthy Subramani, who hosts a popular Tamil-language television program, says that both cow dung and yellow pumpkin flower have the ability to "stop germs at the door" and prevent them from entering the house.

As for the smell, you get used to it, I guess. Stop noticing it. I remember the first time I encountered black truffles at a fancy, now-defunct restaurant at Central Park South. The waiter ceremoniously shaved what looked like charcoal on top of my pasta. It had a weird smell. But everyone was raving about it. I suppose it all depends on your point of view. My relatives, for instance, refuse to touch a fungus that has been dug up by a pig. Unfit for human consumption, they will say. Smells weird, even to me. Humans have invented a wide variety of quirky uses for the fruits of nature—from flora and fauna. What seems natural in one culture horrifies another. The same with cow dung.

Whenever my father's cousin Kicha traveled to the city, where he ate on a dining table instead of on the floor, he carried a bottle containing a greenish liquid. The label read "Mr. Muscle" but it was, in fact, diluted cow dung. He would spray the liquid on the table and instruct the womenfolk to wipe the table. He got away with it—almost. It was the peculiar smell that gave him away. Ever since, every home that he visited had conscientious objectors to his Mr. Muscle bottle. The minute he pulled it out, the hosts objected—strenuously.

As a child, I had several intimate encounters with cows and cow dung. Most fertile of all, in more ways than one, was the house-warming ceremony of my cousin Vikram. It happened in the '80s, when I was a teenager.

Vikram was the oldest cousin, the one all of us teenage girls had a crush on. Brilliant, tall, lanky, he was every Indian mother's vision of the ideal bachelor—or at least the mothers in the Tamil Brahmin community I belong to (shortened to "TamBrahm" in today's slang. Several hearts were crushed when Vikram was admitted to Boston

University for graduate school. When he returned to India one summer, he had rechristened himself "Vic" and asked his father to convert their rambling ancestral home into a modern two-story apartment building. A couple of years later, Vic's apartment was ready—marble floors, white walls, and minimalist furniture.

The entire clan gathered for the housewarming ceremony, complete with priest and feast. Vic appeared in Nike shorts and was promptly instructed to change into the traditional Indian dhoti (sarong). My four uncles, one of whom was Vic's father, wanted a cow to inaugurate the apartment. They bribed the local milk woman, who produced a cow. Using hay, bananas, and jaggery (clumps of unrefined sugar made from date palm and sugarcane), my uncles coaxed the cow up two flights of stairs and straight into Vic's new digs. When he came out of his bedroom clad in a dhoti, Vic encountered a large, slightly angry Brahman cow, and a mildly disapproving Brahmin priest, staring straight at him.

"Can you repeat Sanskrit mantras after me?" asked the priest huffily.

"What is that animal doing here?" asked Vic.

Vic's dad rang the bronze bell to signal that the proceedings could start. Nobody paid Vic any attention. All eyes were on the cow. The priest was instructed to lengthen the mantras to allow time for the cow to give a nice shit.

"We need the cow dung to fall in the house," said an uncle. "It is beneficial."

"No way. Not in this modern apartment," said Vic.

"Silly boy. Cow dung is where goddess Lakshmi resides."

Vic tried the proverbial "over my dead body" approach but the priest's Sanskrit mantras drowned him out.

Nothing happened. The cow stood patiently, lubricated by periodic treats of sugarcane stalks, jaggery, and sweets. One of my uncles had a bright idea and whispered to the others. Two of them took up positions on each side of the cow. They glanced at each other and bent in unison to massage the sides of the cow in an attempt to get it to shit. The surprised cow snorted but was given more sugar to calm it down. After a few minutes of massaging, the cow gave a loud bellow and released enough methane gas to light up a small town. Just as we were recovering from the odor, it dumped olive-green dung, which splattered all over Vic's white marble floor.

My uncles grinned delightedly and began applauding the cow.

Vic stared at his new floor and began muttering "What the fuck! What the fuck! What the fuck!" in time to the Sanskrit chant of the priest.

The priest sped up the proceedings after that.

Once the ceremony ended, a significantly lighter, fairly sugared-up cow trotted down two flights of stairs. The daughters of the family, including me, were pressed into action. Armed with brooms and a plastic dustpan, we were told to scoop up the dung into a large bucket. It smelled (or stank, depending on your proclivities and sensitivities) to high heaven. My uncles wanted to dilute the cow dung with water and sprinkle it all over the house "for purity," but Vic finally put his Nike sneaker–shod foot down. He wouldn't hear of it.

That evening, there was a flaming row between Vic and his father. The details are hazy in my mind, but the theme remains vivid, perhaps because this happens repeatedly in India: the war between five thousand years of tradition and twenty-first-century modernity, the conflict between the Western-educated mind and the Indian soul, a debate that touches many aspects of life ranging from marriage to child-rearing to house-warming and cows.

Elders defend arranged marriages to their US-educated grandchildren. Haircutters defend folk wisdom, such as when to have a haircut, to skeptical software engineers. Don't cut your hair during the waning phase of the moon, they say. Things grow better when the moon waxes. A father defends the use of cow dung to his furious son. Vic was aghast that his father continued to follow "mindless superstitions" that had no basis in science.

"How do you know that it has no basis in science?" asked his father.

And thus the argument began, all over again. It has continued over decades at every family gathering.

Vic couldn't be persuaded to enter the apartment again. He returned to Boston, married a woman named Emily and has lived there happily ever after. His father, who wanted no part of Boston or beef-eating Emily, occupied his apartment, which perhaps was the point of the whole exercise.

"These modern young people don't understand the value of our traditions," said Vic's dad. "We have immersed ourselves in cow products and cow dung for five thousand years. If it was bad for us, you think we would be the second most populous nation on earth?"

ONE DAY, MY NEIGHBOR Rachael and I collect a few of the building's children to teach them about composting and recycling. We stand in front of the giant terra-cotta composting container, surrounded by buckets of just-collected household organic waste. In front of us are a group of dubious-looking kids carrying a basketball.

When I bring up cow manure, the conversation quickly degenerates to exclamations of "Gross!" and "Ewww."

"What's wrong with cow dung?" says Rachael. "Our farmers have used it for centuries. It is part of Indian culture."

Oh no, and here we go, I think. What begins as a composting lesson is quickly deteriorating into a debate on what constitutes Indian culture, played out ad nauseam between generations, including online and on television, without conclusion.

"Cow urine and cow dung may be part of our culture but that doesn't mean that we have to wallow in it," says a nine-year-old.

"Nobody is asking you to wallow in it, smart aleck," I reply. "All we want you guys to realize is that ancient Indians discovered many things about their environment that could well be true."

"Or not," says a teenager. "If cow dung is so great, don't you think some enterprising pharmaceutical company would have bottled it and sold it for a ton of money?"

"Maybe they will," I retort. "Indians have used coconut oil for their hair and skin for generations. And now, just because Gwyneth Paltrow raved about coconut oil, all you girls are applying it to your hair?"

"I thought you'd be happy that I was using coconut oil," my daughter chimes in. "After all, you've been bugging me to oil my hair."

"I *am* happy. Coconut oil, cow dung, it is all part of the Indian experience. The main message here, guys, is that you shouldn't dismiss everything that is native and traditional as 'old-fashioned.' Science may have solved some problems but it also created some."

"Nobody is saying that," says my daughter. "All we are saying is that none of this cow dung shit—and I'm not even going to apologize for swearing because it makes perfect sense in this context—is scientifically proven."

"This is not about cow dung. It is about how you view the world. Indians discovered many things empirically, through trial and error."

And this, ladies and gentlemen, is how you get stuck into positions. You say something to counter a point of view and then have to back it up, digging yourself deeper and deeper into cow shit.

"So what do you want me to do?" asks my daughter. "Do you want me to mix cow dung in water and throw it in our courtyard like you said you did as a kid? Because I am so not going to do that . . . "

It is her snide tone that gets to me. "First of all, we don't have a courtyard," I reply. "Second of all, even if we did, it is not as if every Indian is pouring cow-dung water on their courtyards."

"Aunty, you are contradicting yourself," someone yells. "You just said that you want us to use cow dung."

Everyone starts speaking at the same time.

"You are twisting my words. Okay, have it your way," I say. "Use all those chemicals that you buy in Bath and Body Works. Spray yourself with deodorant and perfume all you want. You guys are too young to be using all these chemicals. When I was your age, I didn't touch cosmetics. I wasn't allowed to use any of the stuff till I was eighteen."

"Oh yeah, you just drank milk and sprayed cow dung all over the house. Ma, we can argue about this till the cows come home . . . "

"Actually, did you know that this whole idea of the 'cows coming home' is a Western one?" I ask. "In India, the cows don't dawdle. They rush home. There is even a time called '*go-dhuli*' that refers to the cows running home to their calves."

"What are you talking about?"

"Well, you know that phrase that you just used: 'We can argue till the cows come home.' That's a Scottish proverb, and it suggests that the cows are languid creatures and take a long time to come home. All I'm saying is that this whole idea of the cows dawdling is a Western concept. In India, it is the opposite. When we describe mighty rivers flowing at great speed, we say that the river 'flowed like a cow rushing towards its calf.'"

The kids have lost interest. They go off to play basketball.

It is true, though. Indian poetry uses the cow as a metaphor to describe speed, fertility, maternal instincts, and a nurturing benevolence. The ancient river Sindhu, also known as the Indus (which gives the Indus Valley Civilization its name), is described as the mightiest of all rivers, the one into which other roaring rivers run "like mothers to their calves," not calves to their mothers, as I first mistakenly thought. Cows are not slow; they are just deliberate. Cow don't linger; they rush to their calves like a river rushes to sea. India's ancient poets knew this.

The Sindhu River—who flows flashing and white, with ample volume; whose roar can be heard to the heavens; who bellows like a bull; and who is beautiful like a steed. Animal metaphors all.

Part Two

12

MY MILK WOMAN
HAS A PROPOSITION

WE STAND ON THE sidewalk and talk, Sarala and I and the other ladies—about schools and recipes; cows and power cuts; babies and bath water. A breeze ruffles our hair. Everyone is relaxed. Noisy parakeets circle a fruiting fig tree nearby. Milk from the cow's udder squirts softly and rhythmically into the large bucket.

Selva carries the bucket of milk to the culvert. We crowd around like bees. Army rookies in khaki half-pants and white vests show up out of nowhere. They thrust their cans to the front of the line. A fight threatens to break out. Sarala placates everyone, speaking in Telugu, Kannada, Tamil, and Hindi by turn.

Sarala has a system. She pours the milk and then adds a little extra; a couple of teaspoons to top it off, as a goodwill gesture— "for joy," as she says. It is a smart marketing tactic. Most of her customers don't pay attention to whether she measures their three or four liters of milk correctly using her well-worn, aluminum measuring cup. But if she doesn't give them the extra *kosuru*, as we call it, people notice. Today, she fails to spoon out my joy.

"Where is my extra *kosuru*?" I complain.

"What to do, Madam?" Sarala replies. "We are short of cows."

THIS IS A PREAMBLE to a proposition. Sarala wants me to buy a cow for her. It will cost about one thousand dollars. Her intention is to pay me back. Over the next few days, Sarala and I go back and forth about her loan or "advance," as people call it here.

The word *advance* sounds more benign than *loan*. For a developing economy such as India, an advance makes eminent sense, given the youthful population. It suggests progress and betterment— latent potential turning into reality. You are advancing your twenty-four-year-old, married driver twelve hundred dollars to help him buy a "two-wheeler," which he will use to transport his family of four. He will return the advance to you in the form of safe driving, daily cleaning of your vehicle, good attitude, and multiple other tangible and intangible variables, and eventually, after a couple of years—you hope—in cash. A loan on the other hand has all kinds of unsavory associations: sharks, defaults, credit, and loan calculators. A loan is cold and cutting. An advance is civilized.

When I moved here, well-meaning friends warned me about the "advance thing," particularly as it applied to hiring household help. It would be only a matter of time before household staff would ask for advances, they said. Best to come up with a strategy.

Collect something as collateral. Register their names with the police or threaten to complain to the cops in case of default. Best of all, simply refuse all requests for advances.

So I did. In the beginning, when I interviewed people to hire, I made loud pronouncements about how I wouldn't give advances. Instead, I would pay above-market rates. That lasted about a week. Sour neighbors called me up and complained that I was messing with the pay scale of the building. Their help was demanding higher salaries because of me.

"If you must pay more, pay 10 or 20 percent more, not like 50 percent," said the building committee treasurer, an accountant by profession.

Strapped by a salary bandwidth, I was forced to consider advances.

"Sometimes I feel like moving back to New York so I don't have to deal with all these advances and salary permutations and complications," I complained to my brother, Shyam.

"Come on, that's like Pa saying that he wants to tear down the house because the toilet is leaking," Shyam replied.

I came up with variations. I told the first woman I hired that I would only give an advance of under a month's salary. She waited a week and asked for four times that amount. She would return it in a year, she said. By then, I liked her work too much to refuse. My first driver borrowed progressively larger amounts until he owed me one thousand dollars, but he always made sure that he paid back something each month. One day he quit without notice or without repaying the four hundred dollars that was left from his loan. I clamped down and stopped giving advances to the ironing man, vegetable vendor, or flower man. That, too, lasted about a week.

I'd like to unleash a psychologist or a behavioral economist to figure out Indian advances, because you know what? There is no model; there is no uniform. One size doesn't fit all. What is true is that it is only a matter of days before the cook, driver, housekeeper, part-time cleaner, gardener, or whoever it is you employ, will ask you for a loan. The size will vary based on several factors: need, circumstance, length of employment, and ability to repay. The cynic in me thinks that the people you hire suss you out and ask for the maximum that they can get away with. They intend to pay it back. Except stuff happens and they have to leave town.

People can be both crafty and noble. In his famous essay "Is There an Indian Way of Thinking," A. K. Ramanujan writes that Indians are adept at holding two contradictory thoughts in our heads. This implies a certain comfort with ambiguity, the gray areas. Children have this ability to hold not just two contradictory thoughts but multiple thoughts at the same time. We call it imagination.

Dualism is not just about quantum theory or world-changing ideas. It works in smaller contexts too. When I argue with Ram, I am usually intent on proving that I am right and he is wrong. India has ground that out of me. I am convinced I am right. He is equally convinced that he is right. Guess what, I tell him one day, we are both right.

He stares at me suspiciously. "Is this you attempting to take the high road or some weird version of it?" he asks.

"No," I reply seriously. "It is just that there is no one truth. It is all perception."

The argument doesn't end but my husband is silenced, at least for the moment.

Living in India, I have learned the art of silence; of letting comments slide without getting all fussed about them. And it's not just arguments or advances—or requests to buy cows. For example, what do you do when an aunt you haven't seen for twenty years greets you at a wedding by saying, "You've developed a paunch"? Or when your mother-in-law's colleague walks into your home for the first time and asks, by way of introduction, "How much did you pay for this apartment?"

When I was first confronted with this particular inquiry from a perfect stranger, I was stumped. I blurted out the cost. Nowadays, I am wiser. When this question is asked, as it often is, I talk about cost per square foot and change the subject.

Over time, you realize that people in India ask questions or make unwieldy comments to fill gaps in conversation, or they ask for the price of your apartment without preamble or introduction because they don't view it as personal. They would gladly volunteer such information about themselves should you be interested. And when an elderly aunt says that you have put on weight, she is trying—however awkwardly—to be affectionate. She has known you since you were a child and merely wants to remind you of how thin you used to be. You should be flattered that she has noticed your weight gain.

Or maybe Indian uncles of a certain age are just ornery, and Indian aunties are hormonal and need estrogen shots. And maybe in these instances sometimes being silent is not the only route. Yes, learn not to take things literally and retain a sense of humor, but also understand when to turn defensive politeness into offensive aggression, matching personal remark for personal remark. In other words, when people call you fat, you call them bald—with a smile and an affectionate hug, of course.

When Sarala keeps asking me to buy bottled water from her son Senthil she doesn't really expect a response. She just can't help trying. And none of her other customers will even entertain such entreaties. "These army folks are like vultures," Sarala will say. "They want the best quality milk but ask them to pay a penny more, they won't agree. They will say that it is beyond their capacity to pay that much for milk."

I am the only fat-cat "bungalow customer" Sarala has. It would be a crime to allow such a circumstance to go unexplored. So she tries a variety of ways to prize money from me. Because she tries it so transparently, it is hard for me to take offense. Plus, I really like her.

I CAN AFFORD TO give Sarala the thousand-dollar loan for a cow, but I don't want her to view me as her sugar daddy, or mommy in this case. So I conjure up elaborate methods to establish my inadequacy. My mother has a simpler approach. She just says no.

One morning, as I stand waiting for the milk, I take out my cell phone and have a long, imaginary conversation in Tamil, which Sarala speaks, with a bank manager who is harassing me about my home loan. I plead to this imaginary man not to raise the interest rates. I tell him that I will definitely pay for the month in two days. Money is short because of a medical emergency, I say. Next month I plan to make it up. While I am having this loud "conversation" entirely for Sarala's benefit, she is talking to the other ladies, seemingly oblivious to my pleas.

In the end I hang up, sigh theatrically, turn to Sarala, and explain the whole imaginary situation again with renewed vigor. "I have a home loan that is hanging like a noose around my head," I end.

Sarala smiles sympathetically. "Everybody has problems," she says, as she has said before. "You have high-rise-size problems. I have hut-size problems."

Finally, I think. She equates herself with me. I am not merely a gravy train.

My husband has a different view. He is shocked that I am contemplating buying a cow.

"The milk lady across the street needs another cow to supplement her income. I thought I would buy her one," I begin.

Ram raises his eyebrows and gives me *the look*. I have to back off. He already thinks I've gone nuts. Well, I was always nuts, but in India, being nuts seems easier. I am, after all, doing a dance-therapy workshop, meeting with schoolmates who are into neuro-linguistic programming (NLP), and looking into past-life regression just because I am curious about it. On top of it all, I have started seeing a shrink.

"You had to wait till we moved to India to see a shrink?" asks Ram. "Why didn't you do this in New York where everything is so much more standardized?"

"Because things are cheaper here," I reply. "I pay, like, five dollars an hour."

"But why do you need to see a shrink?"

I sigh but don't answer. Ever since I received my undergraduate degree in psychology, I have been subject to questions like this. Indians—or should I say, my family—view psychology as a nebulous pursuit, just above the work of witch doctors, shamans, and astrologers.

"Can you read my mind?" was the question I got when I told friends and family in India that I was studying psychology. It got old really quick. I had hoped that things would have changed in the twenty years that I was away, that therapy would now be viewed with respect.

"You know, I am so tired of Indians being so skeptical about psychology, therapy, and counseling," I tell my husband. "All my friends in New York see shrinks. Why are we Indians so suspicious of it?"

Ram has no answer. Neither do my brother, father, mother, or in-laws. They all think they have failed me somehow when I tell them I am seeing a therapist.

"Whatever it is, why don't you talk to us?" asks my dad earnestly. "Are you having any problems at home?"

"Pa," I say, exasperated. "I just want to see what therapy feels like. Is that so bad? I studied it and now I want to experience it. And here in India, I can afford it."

My therapist, Uma, operates from a home in the nearby neighborhood of Frazer Town. I rather wish she had a proper couch where I could lie back and talk about all the Freudian stuff I learned in college. I have to make do with a plastic chair instead. I go once a week. Amidst the din of India, it is great to sit in a quiet room and talk about my feelings and angst, about people and their quirks, about the lack of privacy and the chaos that surrounds me, and about how sometimes I cannot sleep because I am obsessing about milk.

"I have started having pretend conversations on the phone," I say to Uma one day.

She doesn't even raise an eyebrow.

"Who with?"

"Mostly banks and mortgage brokers," I reply. "I make up these imaginary phone calls to signal to the people who work for us that I have money troubles."

"How do these conversations go? And how often do you have them?"

"I had one yesterday when I was with my milk lady. Usually, I just plead on the phone. Maybe I'll say, 'I am so sorry for not paying this month's bank loan, sir. Please don't increase the interest rate.' Things like that. So they feel that I have problems, just as they do."

"And why is that important to you?"

"Well, the inequalities of India really bother me."

"In what way?"

"Well, I have many saris in my closet. My maid and cook probably have five expensive saris. The worst part is that they wear saris everyday and know how to enjoy saris. They tie them well and wear matching flowers in their hair. I'm worried that they will feel terrible every time they fold my clothes because they can't afford clothes like mine."

"So what do you do?"

"I hide my new clothes in a trash bag."

"But won't they discover it someday when you take them out?"

The shrink's endless questions don't help me much. It is my mother who comes to my rescue. She smiles when I tell her about how I hide new clothes to spare my maid's feelings.

"Make your home pleasant so people feel like working there," says my mom. "Don't do silly things like hiding your new clothes."

I nod. I am used to dismissing my mother's advice—and you

could make a case for the inequality of the capitalist system in general—but on a person-to-person level, her argument actually makes some sense.

My shrink does, in the end, also give me some good advice. Her techniques are different from what I studied in college. She has a point of view. I thought that shrinks are not supposed to reveal that. She tells me to revel in my relationships. Humans like connections with other people; they hate being lonely. Life in India is all about relationships, she says. Don't fight it. Enjoy it. And drink warm milk with saffron if you can't sleep.

Still, so many people, like Sarala, haven't been given the same opportunities that I have. I am just plain lucky. It isn't fair and it totally sucks.

13

A COW AS A BIRTHDAY GIFT?

ONE MORNING, SARALA BRINGS a bounding Alsatian puppy on a leash. It belongs to Senthil, she explains. "He is crazy about animals. Brings them home. He has collected a pigeon, parakeets, a cat, and now this puppy."

Sarala's daughter-in-law, apparently, is furious.

"There isn't room in our one-bedroom house for the ten of us, let alone this puppy," says Sarala. "And now we have a newborn baby, too. How will my daughter-in-law adjust to this?"

There is a pause. Might I want an Alsatian? Sarala asks. She knows that I am looking for a puppy.

They want to get rid of the Alsatian but only to a family that will allow them to visit the dog from time to time. "It has to go to a good home. That is the main thing," says Sarala with finality. She looks at me hopefully.

"Alsatians are police dogs," I dither, gazing at the energetic puppy barking for milk. "We are looking for, oh, I don't know, a Labrador or beagle, a softer breed, maybe."

Sarala promises to keep an eye out. She smiles indulgently at the Alsatian. "See how smart he is already. He wants milk," she says. "He knows exactly when the milk is ready."

They eventually give the puppy to an army man who has a large compound for the high-spirited dog to run around in.

Over the next several weeks, Sarala takes me to see several dog breeders. Through her network of connections, we buy a ginger-colored Labrador puppy, much to the delight of my children. We name her Inji, which means "ginger" in Tamil.

Inji, while still just a few months old, refuses to leave our apartment complex. Walking on the road terrifies her: her tail goes between her legs and she simply sits down in stubborn defiance. There are many reasons for Inji's antiwalking stance—most have to do with me. On one or two memorable occasions, I royally chewed her out on the road because she hadn't done her business after half an hour of walking. One time, I got so fed up that I dropped her leash in protest. She ran away, banged against a cyclist who fell on top of her, and created pandemonium all around. House training my puppy, like many things in my life, has shown me exactly how inadequate I am.

We have newspapers all over the floor and have to strategize about how to get the puppy out the door for walks. It is chaos. This is at odds with what my husband wants from life. Ram wants to name our home *Samatvam*. This Sanskrit word—the closest

English translation is "equanimity"—encompasses much of what he aspires to. *Aspires* being the operative word here, because actually both my husband and I are samatvam wannabes. We want to project Zen-like calm during crises, which we do, but then we end up losing it for the most pedestrian and idiotic of reasons.

Through the Bhagavad Gita, Hinduism advocates equanimity in no uncertain terms. One of the Gita's most famous verses teaches that you can control your actions, not the results. Yoga, in its simplest and most lofty sense, means samatvam—"samatvam yoga uchyathe," as the verse goes: "Yoga means equanimity."

To this profound assertion, I add my own method of attaining equanimity—get a puppy. Even though in the beginning there is pandemonium, in a roundabout way—and I think Ram would agree—Inji has taught us much about achieving samatvam.

What distinguishes animal lovers is the belief that animals understand what we say and who we are, not just in the superficial listening-to-orders sense, but in the deepest intuitive sense. After several months of getting trained by my puppy, I have gone from skeptic to believer. I think my dog is an excellent mirror of my emotions. When I am calm, she is calm. When I am angry, she is sad. When I am happy, she is happy. And when I am samatvam— as in, when I don't scold her for small lapses like urinating on my carpet, she blossoms. Her spirit unfurls. Me samatvam; she samatvam. Or is it the reverse?

Sarala adds one more item to the toolkit of "how to get the dog to walk on the road."

"Animals calm each other down, Madam. Once you get a cow, you will calm down and therefore your puppy will calm down, too," she says.

I *have* calmed down, though. In many ways, my interactions with Sarala are healing. I tell her all my problems with the house, with my writing, and with family. I have stopped going to the shrink. That, according to Ram, is Sarala's biggest contribution to my life. She has turned into my therapist.

BOTH MY FATHER AND father-in-law are celebrating their eightieth birthdays in a few months with grand Hindu ceremonies that last three days. The ceremony is called *Sathabhishekam* and occurs after a man has seen one thousand full moons per the lunar calendar, which I think works out to completing eighty years, eight months, and eight days.

A big part of the celebration is contributing alms to Brahmins. While going through the list of donations with our family priest, one of the rituals that keeps coming up is *go-dhaan*, or "cow-donation," which is considered to be very auspicious. Hindus offer many reasons for why they consider the cow important. Some of it has to do with the Lord Krishna, the primeval cowherd, who played his flute and attracted the cows to him. Many of his names are linked with cows, for instance: Govinda—one who brings pleasure and satisfaction to cows; Gopala—one who protects cows.

Krishna grew up in Gokulam (another cow linkage) and is the inspiration for many schools of art, music, and dance in India. There are miniature paintings of him with cows, stories about how he knew each of his cows by name and sight, and how he had 108 herds of cows separated by color and had different names for each type. Hindu Indians who have the means don't need any persuasion about go-dhaan. My mother, for example, has been wanting to do this for years. Every time I bring up charity, she talks about cow-donation in the same breath as contributing to CARE.

For me, this comes as some sort of cosmic synchronicity. I have gone through a series of mental shifts with respect to buying a cow for Sarala: first suspicion, then curiosity, then a tentative decision to loan her the money, then figuring out if she could and would return my loan, and then moving to my current state—rationalization. Even if Sarala wanted to, it is highly unlikely that she can pay me back such a large amount, and maybe that is okay.

Ram and I have been talking about this for weeks. After his initial shock, Ram, too, has warmed to the idea. He sees Sarala as a micro-enterprise that we can help fund.

"You know, the real thing that we need to help Sarala with is improving milk yield per cow," says Ram. "In the US, each cow gives five times as much milk as our Indian cows. It has to do with nutrition."

Ram sees Sarala as an honest, hardworking entrepreneur. Over several weeks of back and forth, we come to terms with "writing off the loan," as he says.

With our fathers' eightieth birthdays, a new option has presented itself. Maybe it isn't a loan but a donation—one that will make all parties happy.

"I am thinking of buying a cow for your birthday," I tell my father-in-law. My in-laws are visiting from their home in Kerala. My father-in-law sits at the head of the dining table, sipping his morning coffee. The morning light shines through the rafters.

I love my apartment. It has bright-yellow walls and an antique wooden swing, about the size of a single bed, in the middle of the living room. The colors of my home in Bangalore are completely and vibrantly Indian: peacock blue, parrot green, vermilion red, mango yellow, and mahogany brown.

My father-in-law looks up from his newspaper but doesn't blink.

"Well, it is better than buying you ten packets of Proteinex or Ensure, which is what I was going to buy you," I say defensively.

My father-in-law has become frail. He's been an asthmatic for many years, and his lungs are troubling him, making him breathless and dependent on steroids and nebulizers. We are pressing my in-laws to rent an apartment in our building to be near us, setting his upcoming birthday as an informal move date.

My father-in-law doesn't want a thing for his milestone birthday. No golf vacations—he doesn't play golf. No cruise—he had traveled the world while working in the Indian civil service for two prime ministers, Indira Gandhi and Morarji Desai. Now he just wants to stay home and catch up on all the books that he has been meaning to read over the years. But if I want to give him a cow for his birthday, so be it.

I say the same thing to my father and get pretty much the same reaction. Donating a cow is a good thing. If that makes me happy, why not?

THE QUESTION IS, WHICH COW? The priest says that it has to be a native breed, although we will end up fudging that a bit. But which kind? Which color? What personality? Just as Eskimos have multiple names for ice and Romani have scores of names for clouds, ancient Indians had beautiful names to describe the color of cows.

Not just the usual white, black, and brown cows, but also cows that were *dhumra* (smoke-colored); *palala dhumra* (the color of smoke that rises from burning hay); *vata renu suvarna* (the color of dust that is raised by the wind); *pinga* (reddish-brown); and *gowri* (yellow-colored cow). Gifting cows of various colors brought a variety of merits. A white cow appeases the god of water, Varuna. A gold-colored cow naturally influences Kubera, the god of wealth. Some are less obvious. Gifting a black cow appeases the lord of fire, Agni; a white one is for Indra, king of the gods. A smoky cow pleases Yama, the god of death. Sanskrit literature is full of instructions about whether to gift a cow that is with calf or not. I turn, not to Sanskrit, but to my native village.

Every Indian has an ancestral village where he "hails" from, as we say. This is the village where you trace your family tree going back ten generations; where your family deity, often of tribal origin, makes its home; and where you make annual pilgrimages to propitiate your tribal god or goddess so that your clan can thrive.

These "antecedents," as Indians often say, give us very specific idiosyncrasies and unstated enmities, deep-seated but cleverly hidden superiority complexes—each of us believes that the patch of land from which we sprung makes us better than everybody else—combined with a chip on the shoulder towards our neighbors, who we know harbor the same opinions (or delusions, hence the insecurity) of themselves. Strip away the politeness; strip away the genuine belief in plurality, the abhorrence of "narrow domestic walls," as poet Rabindranath Tagore calls it; strip away the garden-party persona and pour a few dirty martinis, and then ask me who I am and I will tell you, somewhat sheepishly, perhaps bolstered by some Carnatic instrumental music, that I am a TamBrahm. Really, the music is key. Django Reinhardt or Manitas de Plata will not produce the same sense of local pride.

My father's side hails from a village in Palghat, where the deity is the goddess Panchali—she of five husbands. Pretty neat, I thought as I studied Mughal kings with their harems in history lessons. My goddess had the male version of a harem. Every summer my family and I visited our native village to worship the goddess and spend time with relatives who lived there. Before going, my father would call his second cousin Kicha (he of Mr. Muscle fame) to "apprise him of our arrival," said Dad, but really so that they would have breakfast ready when our train arrived at 5 a.m. My mother always carried gifts: talcum powder, mirrors of different shapes, saris in the latest "city fashions," and select medicines for bacterial infections. Naturally, we were welcomed with joy.

Still, at first these visits were awkward for my city-born-and-bred brother and me. We grew up in Chennai, which was called Madras when we lived there. We thought we had little in common with these folks who claimed a kinship with us. Over the years, we warmed to the experience and grew to enjoy these trips. They had a rustic simplicity to them, these folks, which put a child at ease. There was none of that stilted city formality. Nobody waited for introductions before speaking to us. They simply enveloped us in a hug and proceeded to talk as if we had never left the village.

The most fantastic cow story I've heard came during one of these trips. Apparently, my great-grandmother was trying to get pregnant without success. The family astrologer was summoned. He created charts, threw cowrie shells, and looked at omens. He said that my great-grandmother had *sarpa-dosham*, or the curse of a serpent. She had probably killed one in her past life, so now the serpent was "eating up all the eggs" that grew in her womb. This was why she was having trouble conceiving. The next morning, the family cow was nowhere to be found. The family searched throughout the village for her. Finally, they spotted her on the outskirts of town. She was standing over a rocky outcrop. Milk was flowing out of her udder and into the holes where serpents lived.

"She was trying to propitiate the serpent lord, you see," said Kicha, "so that he would remove the curse from our family. Now, how did a cow know this? Who knows? But it worked. The next month, your great grandmother got pregnant and delivered a bonny baby boy. If the cow hadn't done what she did, we would all not be here. I wouldn't be talking to you."

Now that I am back in India, I decide to accompany my parents on their annual visit to our native village. On the way there, I tell my dad my idea of donating a cow in honor of his upcoming birthday. His reaction is much like Ram's father's—fine, if that's what we want to do. We have met our relatives, eaten lunch, taken a siesta, and are at the Panchali Amman temple for the evening *darshan* (viewing). The priest at the temple has that polite, focused aggressiveness that is sometimes common amongst touts. He probably gets a commission every time he snags a donation. My parents tell him that we are considering donating a cow.

"You know how children are. They want to do the best for us," says my dad, suddenly chuffed with pride. "They are insisting on a cow in honor of my eightieth birthday."

"And why not?" asks the priest. "That is the duty of children—to do what is best for the parents, the family, and the lineage. You have raised them well."

Compliments out of the way, we get down to brass tacks.

There are two options, says the priest. Poor people choose the partial donation. For fifteen hundred rupees, or about twenty-five dollars, we can buy a "share" in the temple cow and participate in all the Hindu rituals involved with cow donation. The temple cow, naturally, is returned to the temple. In effect, it is a recycled cow.

The other option is to purchase the "full package," where we can actually buy a cow and its calf, and donate them to a poor Brahmin family. We would cap the cow's horns with silver bells, buy a colorful cloth to put over its back, and then walk it to a village where we would ceremoniously donate it to the family. We would be responsible for all the feed (the cow's, not the family's) for a year and the family would have the asset—both the capital in the form of the cow and the dividends in the form of its milk—for its lifetime. The approximate cost: sixteen hundred dollars.

"Buying a share of the temple cow is far less expensive but you won't get the complete spiritual benefit," says the priest, gauging our reactions with a keen eye to see which way we are leaning.

While it is true that my advancing the money for Sarala to buy a cow is not the same as donating the cow to her, I decide that it's a trivial difference. I assume that Sarala's request is proof that the universe is conspiring with the events that are happening in our family. By squaring this away in my head as an act of charity, I know that I won't get too sad if Sarala doesn't return my money. Ram agrees. Even though they make light of it, we know that both our fathers will feel happy about the cow donation, which as it turns out has come to us serendipitously through Sarala. Why not do it?

There is only one more snag. The cow has to be donated to a Brahmin. Hindu literature is quite firm about that. The *Garuda*

Purana, in which Lord Vishnu turns into an eagle named Garuda and narrates an eight-hundred-page tome that covers things as varied as the "cosmogeny of hell and other regions; modes of spiritual initiation; a brief discourse on yoga; installation of divine images; discourses on royal strategies to appease the gods presiding deities of the different planets and constellation of stars; situations of yoginis on the different days of the fortnight; description of gems and their uses."

The *Garuda Purana* is categorical about how to donate a cow: "Gifts of cows, proprietary rights in lands, food grains and gold, should be given to a Brahmin, who is in every way worthy of receiving the same. A Brahmin who has neither erudition nor is a seeker of spiritual knowledge has no right to accept any gifts; and degrades the giver as well as his own soul by accepting any."

All roads, it seems, point to Brahmins.

The priest agrees vehemently with the tome. "It isn't an act of charity unless you donate said cow to a Brahmin," he says.

Sarala, I know, is no Brahmin. She belongs to the Naidu caste.

Caste is one of India's enduring contradictions. For some, it is a marker of identity, one that they have inherited through birth and family. You are born into one of four castes: Brahmin (priests), Kshatriya (warriors), Vaishya (merchants), or Shudra (sweepers). Within these broad divisions is a dizzying array of sub-castes. Plus, their names vary regionally. Naidus are one sub-caste of the merchant caste.

I was born a Brahmin. In today's India, however, caste is in flux. Most of my friends have "inter-caste" marriages where, say, a Brahmin has married a Vaishya. Some marry across religions—Christians and Muslims marrying Hindus. My driver, for instance, is a Hindu. His wife is Christian. He asks for days off on both Christmas and Diwali.

"Why must I donate a cow only to a Brahmin?" I ask the priest.

"It is tradition," he replies. "Brahmins took care of cows, used the milk and other offerings in their rituals."

I consider arguing with him. Actually, I want to say, the dairy farmers of India belong to a variety of castes, not just Brahmin. Plus, the people who take care of cows across my street are Naidus.

But I know it is futile. I cannot fight a thousand years of tradition by espousing a different point of view, however well thought out it may be.

What to do? I consider asking the Brahmins in my community if they will receive the cow from me before passing it on to Sarala. But it won't work. Even if I can legally prove that I have donated the cow to a Brahmin, the Gods will know that Sarala is the end user. But do Hindu gods embrace the caste system that I disagree with?

As a nominal Hindu, I have many quarrels with the religion I was raised with. For one, it is patriarchal. Which the feminist in me resents. A lot of the mantras aren't supposed to be recited by women. The priests are all men. Only men are honored with milestone events celebrated with great pomp. Witness the grand birthday celebrations that we are putting together for our fathers. Most Hindu women don't celebrate their eightieth birthday with three days of rituals involving a dozen priests and the donation of food, clothing, cows, and cash. After mulling over all this, I decide that the key word in this hoary Hindu prescription is "deserving," not "Brahmin."

That, Sarala is.

14

CAUSE AND COLLATERAL

HINDUS DIDN'T ALWAYS VENERATE cows. In fact, they ate beef, even the ancient pious Hindus who gave us the Vedas and Upanishads. The first time I mentioned this, I almost got thrown out of a family wedding.

"Don't talk nonsense," said an elderly uncle. "The cow has been sacred in India for thousands of years."

"I told you that you shouldn't send your daughter to America," an aunt accused my mother. "Look at all these crazy, half-baked ideas that she has come up with."

The truth is that while Sanskritists and environmentalists both acknowledge the importance of the native cow, they aren't all in agreement about how Vedic Indians treated this animal. The Vedas speak fondly of the cow in many passages. One passage says that the cow is considered inviolable, *aghnya,* or "not to be slain." And yet most scholars concur that Vedic Indians ate animal flesh, including beef. Something my elderly uncle and aunt could not reconcile when I suggested as much. But ancient Indians differentiated between a sterile cow that could be sacrificed and a milch cow that could not be touched. Milch cows were the mothers of gods; described as "the mother of the Rudras, the daughter of the Vasus, the sister of the Adityas, and the center of nectar."

"Read the *Shatapatha Brahmana,*" says my family's priest. "It will tell you all about why the cow is important."

Written during the Iron Age, between the eighth and sixth centuries BC, the *Shatapatha Brahmana* is a text that gives a long line of injunctions about how to perform fire rituals and sacrifices, how to prepare an altar, how to sit, how to smoke the fire, what to eat, and even how to breathe. Two passages instruct people not to eat the flesh of a cow or an ox, because "verily the cow and the ox support everything here." Other ancient books like the *Apasthamba Dharmasutra* lay a "general embargo on the eating of cow's flesh," to quote an essay by B. R. Ambedkar, the man who was the principal architect of the Indian constitution.

Yet many of these sacred books are full of confusing and occasionally contradictory messages. There are passages exhorting people not to kill or eat cows and oxen. Yet there is a controversial section in the *Shatapatha Brahmana* in which the sage Yajnavalkya, the main priest for the Vedic Indians, says, "I for one eat it (beef), provided it is tender." There are scholars who believe that the Sanskrit translation is wrong; that the word *amsala* used to denote flesh actually means "nourishing flesh" rather than "tender flesh." Still, there seems to be a broad agreement that Vedic Indians ate meat.

Later Vedic rituals and mantras followed the same pattern. Beef-eating was both practiced and censured. Different bovines were sacrificed for different gods: a dwarf cow for Vishnu; a droopy horned ox with a white smear on its forehead for Indra; a red cow for Rudra. All of which suggests that Vedic Indians treated the cow both as a utilitarian animal and as a sacramental object that they used and killed for sacrifices to appease the gods. It was during this time that scores of cows, oxen, goats, and sheep were slain and eaten both as a matter of course and a matter of ritual.

Take a simple custom like welcoming honored guests into your home. There are voluminous texts called sutras, which according to D. R. Bhandarkar, an authority on Indian thought, refers to "manuals of conduct in domestic and social relations." In other words, etiquette books that touch upon, among other things, how to treat honored guests. The Vedic Indians offered *madhuparka* (a mixture of honey and yogurt). Okay, not necessarily my thing, but nice enough.

Then, as Bhandarkar writes in his book, *Some Aspects of Ancient Indian Culture*, a live cow was brought out for the guest who mumbled, "*Hato ma papma; papma me hatah*," or "Destroyed be my sin; my sin be destroyed." After which the honored guest could ask that the cow be slain and the flesh be shared or he could choose that the cow be released in which case the host had to produce another animal for the killing.

Another word for *honored guest* in Sanskrit is *goghna*, which, as Bhandarkar points out, comes from a combination of "to kill" and "a cow." A guest is someone for whom you kill a cow. Sterile cows were killed during weddings and death ceremonies. Bulls were speared and killed; cows were cut with a sword or axe.

So when did they stop killing cows? I guess when they figured out that cows were more useful alive than dead. In her book *The Hindus: An Alternative History,* Wendy Doniger cites a story that suggests how this change happened. In Hindu mythology, a king called Prithu chases Mother Earth, called Prithvi, so that she will provide nourishment for his people. Prithvi assumes the form of a speckled cow and runs away. When the king chases her down, she begs for mercy, and says that she will allow him to milk her for all her products—that she will provide nourishment to his people. And then the earth cow turns into the wishing cow (Kamadhenu: she who grants all wishes, not just food but every earthly sustenance possible).

One day Sarala invites me to see Senthil's shop. Though he hasn't given up the bottled-water venture, her eldest son is now into a new business. It's called Grace Fancy Dress Rental. It is on the first floor of a busy street, about half an hour from my home. Sarala walks into the cramped shop, which has less space than a New York City dry cleaner, and smiles genially at the shop assistant. The sides of the shop are stuffed with black witch hats, purple angel wings, pink tiaras, rhinestone-studded dresses, and khaki uniforms—all child-size. These are costumes that Bangalore schools rent for their annual shows and concerts. There are wigs of all colors and lengths, orange tiger costumes, stitched purple saris, a bunch of neon-green peasant skirts of the kind that my daughter and her classmates wear for their folk dances, in which they pretend to be Bavarians. There are Nehru caps, Gandhi glasses, and Indian flags.

"If your daughters' school needs costumes for their school plays or concerts, you let me know. I'll get you a good rate from my son," says Sarala. Like I said, she can't help trying. We chat for a few minutes with the shop assistant. Senthil, we are told, is out delivering bottled water.

There is a reason Sarala has taken me to her son's shop. It is her collateral. She wants me to know that she can make good on her promise that she will return my money. Her son can sell fancy dresses and Halloween costumes to repay me for the cow that I am going to buy for her.

Ram and I have debated whether to tell her that we are donating a cow to her, not loaning her money. We have decided to keep her in the dark about this mind-shift for now. If she knows that we plan to give her a cow, maybe she will deliberately choose a more expensive breed. That is my reason for caution, anyway. So for now, I keep quiet.

SARALA'S SON SELVA IS surlier than Senthil. Usually clad in a blue blazer and trousers, he is silent as he works with his mother. But he knows his cows. He milks them every morning, and carries the milk pail to the culvert. Sarala takes over the customer service from there. On the odd day when Sarala is not present, Selva stands behind the large milk can, gruffly asking customers if they want one liter or two. We all miss Sarala's smiles and inquiries.

These days, however, I find myself talking to Selva a lot. Sarala trusts her son's opinion when it comes to buying cows and she has gotten him involved in our discussions. He is her cow whisperer, the son who chose a life with these animals in spite of every in-junction otherwise.

"Why don't we go look for a suitable cow?" I say. "If we find the right cow at the right price, I will buy it. If it costs more than one thousand dollars, though, what will you do?" I have already told Sarala I will not advance her more than that.

Selva nods airily in the direction of the bank nearby. He will ar-range something, he says. He has told a couple of friends about his need for a new cow. They have promised to supplement my loan. He wants to finish the deal in two days. This surprises me.

"It is a large sum," I hedge. I feel like a venture capitalist asking a hundred questions before an investment. These questions have no meaning for Selva, caught up as he is in the daily grind of milking, feeding, cleaning, and walking his cows.

Buying a cow is serious business and I had assumed that Selva would engage in the exercise with much deliberation. Yet, here he is, wanting to transact in a mere two days. Is this lack of judgment, lack of time, fear that I will back out of the deal, or confidence that comes from expertise? The speed of this operation scares me. I had envisaged spending a week searching for the right cow, going from village to village, talking to prospective sellers.

Later that week, Sarala tries to calm me down and help make sense of Selva's haste. Selva cannot take off that kind of time, she says. And I realize that cows—live cows—can't be put on hold while he is off gallivanting around villages. This isn't a call center that can be shut down for a week. Every day that he doesn't clean the cowshed has a cost to their family. He has to hire someone to take care of his animals. Selva plans to look for a cow one day and bring it home the next. Two days are all he has. That's it.

We discuss the nitty-gritty. Do we scout out villages for potential cows? Selva has friends who are auto-drivers, he says, and they will take us around. If we show up in my car, the price of the cow will go up.

I offer to pay the rickshaw charges as well. I want to write about cows for the paper I work for I tell them. I explain the journalistic process to them. I'll follow them around, I say. I may take photographs, quote them in my article. Selva interrupts me.

"Write whatever you want," he says. They don't care.

Later that week, a photographer from the English-language newspaper I work for comes and takes pictures of Sarala, Selva, Naidu, and their cows. And when the series of eight articles has been published, I walk across the street and show all three of them all of the newspapers. They look at the photographs but cannot read the words. I translate and explain. They are intrigued but unimpressed. At first, I am a bit hurt by their lack of obvious interest. It occurs to me, though, that for Sarala being featured in an English-language newspaper is about as distant as having a planet named after me (which actually happened for a young Indian girl who was also featured in the paper). I thought, "How cool," but it really wasn't relevant to my life.

The next month, a man from Delhi writes to me and offers to contribute to Sarala's cows. He keeps his word. I take the businessman from Delhi to meet Sarala and pass on the twenty-five thousand rupees that he gives her for cow feed.

It will take another four years for Sarala's story to become a book. When I tell her about my publishing contract, Sarala nods encouragingly. "See how your fortune has changed after you became associated with my cows?" she asks. "That is what is called a cow's blessing, Madam. Show your thanks to these animals by giving them bananas every week."

15

TO MARKET, TO MARKET,
TO BUY A FAT COW

WE SET OUT IN a rickshaw—Sarala, Selva, and I. Sarala would like us to make this trip on an auspicious day, preferably Tuesday or Thursday, but at this point, she doesn't want to add an astrological complication into an already volatile situation.

Selva and I have been bickering for days because he suggests trips first thing in the morning. "Shall we go today?" he asks as I collect milk. I need notice, I say. I can't drop everything to go cow shopping.

Then he adds irritation to my impatience by saying that he will go on his bike to scout out potential cows and take me for the final bidding. I only need to come to pay the money and finish the deal. But I insist that I want to be involved from the very beginning. If I am putting up twelve hundred dollars—the price of the cow has somehow increased in the intervening week—I want to make darn sure that it is a good cow. We go back and forth, squabbling like kids.

Finally, we agree upon a day, and at 10 a.m. we are standing outside my building, waiting for their friend Kuppa, a rickshaw driver, to show up. A few phone calls later, we are on our way to Thanisandra village, close to Bangalore's new airport. We take a turn into a narrow lane from a bustling main road and suddenly the vibes are different. People walk slower. Courtyards have green cow dung splashed over them, with kolam designs as decoration. Cows stand outside buildings. Women in housecoats lay red chilies out to dry.

We drive to a home where a cow is on sale for eight hundred dollars. It is a brown cow with a slight hump. The cow is of medium build and kept in a nice room inside the house. Selva walks the cow around while discussing how much milk it will give. Muniappa, the seller, clad in a white dhoti, shirt, and turban, says that the cow gives twenty liters per day and then quickly modifies it to seventeen liters per day.

This, I know, is a barefaced lie. The average Indian cow gives four to eight liters per day, tops. In the past, says Sarala, when they bought cows they would come during milking time just to make sure that the cow was giving the milk that the seller said it would. Nowadays, everything is too far away and everyone is too busy.

Selva can tell a cow's health simply by looking at its teeth and tail. "Cows should wag their tails," he asserts. "That's how we know they are relaxed."

We walk away after some time. Selva tells me that he doesn't want this cow. It is an Indian breed, a reddish-brown Sindhi cow.

Selva is bent on buying a Holstein-Friesian (HF), a hybrid. They cost more, but they give more milk. That is the assumption, anyway.

"Then did we waste time looking at this cow?" I hiss.

"Just because you want a polyester sari doesn't mean you cannot look at a Kanjivaram silk," replies Sarala.

To put it another way, just because you want the functionality of a Zara dress doesn't mean that you cannot enjoy checking out a Valentino or Chanel outfit.

Selva has another, somewhat shocking reason: manners. "We can't just glance at a cow and walk out," he says. "It is disrespectful to the animal. Even if I am not going to buy it, I have to at least give it the courtesy of a thorough inspection."

This from a guy who is uniformly surly to all humans. I guess his parameters of what constitute good comportment are different for cows.

Muniappa offers us milk. Sarala says that we must accept or he will feel bad. Manners, again. So we drink piping hot cow's milk and start to take our leave. At the last minute, Muniappa jumps into the rickshaw. He knows someone nearby who is selling cows, he says. If he cannot be our seller, he wants to at least be our broker.

Muniappa rides with Kuppa in the driver's seat. He takes us to a mango orchard nearby. We have to stop the rickshaw and walk the final five minutes through narrow village paths. Finally, we see the cows—a dozen of them—grazing underneath trees filled with green mangoes. Some mangoes have exploded on the ground. Their scent perfumes the air. Cows lie in the shade, chewing their cud. They are the epitome of rural contentment, except we are still technically in the city.

Sarala is elated. "Look at these beauties," she mutters. "This is how cows should live. Look at them, how free they are. Their milk will be really tasty because they are so happy."

Selva, too, is suddenly animated. We walk through the shady orchard, examining the cows. Selva grabs some of them, opens their mouths, and stares at their teeth. He pulls and lifts their tails.

All the cows are HF, so their milk production will likely be about the same. Then comes the complicated process of establishing their personalities.

"We have to be careful to buy a cow that is suited to our own dispositions, Madam," says Sarala. "Otherwise, these cows will simply take charge."

Sarala and Selva assess cows using a few informal measures. Two cows lying beside each other are viewed benignly because they will fit into the herd. "Look at that cow licking the other cow," says Sarala, pointing to a pair. "That means that she is naturally easygoing, willing to adjust."

The cow that stares at us curiously is better than the cows that don't even look in our direction. "We want animals that are inquisitive; interested in new things. How else will they adapt in a new home? Some of them pine for their old home and won't eat for days. How will the milk come out if they don't eat?"

Sarala is worried about buying any cow from such a pristine natural environment because her cowshed is quite literally a dump. She is sure that no cow used to such verdant, broad surroundings will like her cowshed. "Why would you leave a palace like this and live in a hovel?" she asks.

Most of the cows are sunning themselves, enjoying the warmth on their backs and staring into space. "What are they thinking?" I wonder aloud.

As always, Sarala has an answer for everything. "Cows are like Buddha, Madam," she says. "They can meditate for hours. Just sitting in one spot. Absorbing the sun's rays."

I thought only native cows absorbed the sun's rays.

"All cows absorb the sun's rays," says Sarala. "Only native cows know what to do with them. Look at these HF cows. They are happily relaxing under the sun, as if this were a beach."

Right on cue, the fighting begins. One cow nudges another cow out of its spot. "Hey, hey," says Selva reflexively, sensing a conflict breaking out. And it does. Both the cows face each other with bowed heads and try to ram their horns into each other.

"People think that all cows are peaceful," says the running commentator standing beside me. "Look at those two. Like wildcats. Imagine what they will do to my peaceful herd. No way we can buy those two."

Each cow has individual characteristics. Some are questioning; some are aggressive; some are emotionally volatile; and some are beatific—they seek simple pleasures. They lie in the sun and raise their heads to smell the air. They chew on wet grass with visible pleasure.

We are eager to transact. Muniappa phones the owner of these cows. After some time, an elderly gent rides up on his moped, clad in the white dhoti, white shirt, and white turban that seem to be the uniform in these parts. He parks the bike, jumps off, all in one quick motion, and says immediately, "No selling."

They cut to the chase, these guys. I've noticed that. Niceties are for people with time, and milk producers don't really have that luxury at their disposal. It is repetitive work that never stops. Right now, at noon, Selva would be cleaning cow dung and getting buckets of water ready for his cows, were he at home. Instead here we are, negotiating with the elderly man, whose name is Ranganna.

"I am keeping these cows," Ranganna says. With his white stubble, gray hair, and lined face, he looks about sixty, but he is probably younger. "They are for my grandson."

Animated discussion breaks out. There seems to be some misunderstanding. Our broker wraps his arm around the potential seller's shoulder, leads him aside, and talks earnestly, massaging his arm the whole time. Even from a distance, we can see our seller shake his head repeatedly.

Ranganna makes a living selling his cows' milk to the local dairy cooperative. He doesn't want to sell his cows, he tells us. He only wants to outsource the milking process. He is fed up with waking up at dawn, squatting beside a dozen cows, and carrying the milk to the local cooperative to be weighed and purchased. He wants a younger man to take over and give his arthritic knees a rest. Would Selva be interested in leasing the cows and subcontracting the milking?

Twice a day Ranganna takes the milk from his twelve cows to the local Karnataka Cooperative Milk Producers' Federation (KMF)—much like the one Sarala and I visited a while back—and sells it for fifty cents per liter, about one-third less than what he would get if he sold it directly to consumers. The milk collected from various independent milk producers is combined and taken to rapid cooling plants where it is homogenized and poured into sealed plastic packets. It is these packets that arrive at my local Nandini Milk Booth, from where my milkman picks them up to deliver them across the city. The milk booth is located—ironically—right in front of the cowshed in which Sarala bolts a couple of her cows at night.

Sarala, according to the state of Karnataka, is an independent milk producer. She prefers to sell directly to consumers for a premium price. Sarala has in theory a great business model and makes more money than the average dairy farmer. Yet because Sarala is not insured, a sick cow or family member throws the household finances completely out of whack. The family is perpetually in debt.

Ranganna doesn't have to spend as much time as Sarala does interacting with and cultivating customers. Besides, everyone in his village has cows. Milk is abundant; customers are not. The cooperative is the only option if he wants to sell his milk.

He asks Selva if the lad will take over milking operations for a monthly salary.

Selva says no. He lives too far away. He cannot drive an hour just to be a paid milker of the elderly man's cows. He wants movable assets, not a job.

We are at an impasse. We plead with the man to no avail. He is polite but firm.

The four of us get back in the rickshaw and bounce along the winding, country paths. By now it is 1 p.m. We are disgruntled, starving, and thirsty. We see a turbaned man selling coconut water by the side of the road. In front of him is a pile of green coconuts. Selva magnanimously offers to buy us all tender coconut water. As the vendor chops off the tops of the coconut, Selva and I continue squabbling about the wasted morning. Why wouldn't he phone first and check with the seller if he were indeed selling his cows, I ask.

Selva blames Muniappa, who blames the old gent for backing out.

"That old man told me that he wanted to sell the whole herd," says Muniappa. "He must have seen this pant-and-shirt Madam and changed his mind."

They all look at me accusingly. The worst part is that I am not wearing Western clothes with their attendant stereotype of a modern and occasionally foreign city-dweller who doesn't "get" what they are about. I am in a traditional sari, trying to blend in.

"You want a cow?" asks the dusty, thin coconut vendor.

We look up.

Turns out that the coconut vendor has a cow that he wants to sell for thirteen hundred dollars. He promises to throw in her calf. Where is the cow? we ask skeptically. The coconut vendor waves at the palatial green mansion, standing like a neon gingerbread house amidst the distant fields. That's my home, he says. Just walk down this path and find my wife. She'll show you the cow and calf.

We stare at each other, jaws agape. They all speak together in rapid-fire Kannada. At the end, Selva seems satisfied that the coconut vendor indeed has a cow. We get back in the rickshaw. Kuppa makes a U-turn and we go in the face of oncoming traffic till we suddenly veer off into a side lane.

Sarala and I can't stop talking about the coconut seller. We are wonderstruck that this dusty, bony man selling coconuts by the roadside has not only a large mansion with fields all around but also saleable cows, to boot.

"Why would a man who owns this giant green mansion, fields, and cows want to sell coconuts by the roadside?" I ask in amazement.

"He must have seen all those coconuts on his land going to waste so he probably thought, 'Why not stand on the road and make some more money?'" says Selva.

We walk single file in between the fields and go to the green mansion. An old man comes out. He is the coconut vendor's father and has the leathery skin of a man who has spent his lifetime outside under the hot sun. When we ask about the cow, he points to the field and says that we will find the animal there, with his daughter-in-law. Selva walks into the tall sugarcane field, whistles, and returns.

In a few minutes, a woman clad in an orange sari comes out. Had I passed her on the road, I would have pegged her (correctly) as a farmer's wife. I would certainly not have imagined that she was the owner of the green, two-story house, about the size of my suburban split-level in Stamford, Connecticut, spread over ten thousand feet of virgin Bangalore land.

The coconut vendor's wife leads out her cow. Selva does his thing with examining the teeth and tail. As we walk back to our car, he tells Sarala that he is going to try to negotiate down the price to twelve hundred dollars. He is not hopeful, though.

"These sellers may lower the price by 10 percent, but no more. The cow is young and healthy. Plus there is a calf. The seller is not in dire straits," says Selva, waving at the green house. "Why will he lower the price?"

His logic is impeccable. We motor back to the coconut vendor. As predicted, he refuses to lower the price.

"I didn't even plan on selling my cow," he says. "Just because you people came here with such distress, I thought I'd do you a favor by offering my cow."

And that is the end of that.

By now it is 3 p.m. None of us has eaten. On the way home, we pass a roadside stand where Selva treats us to some masala peanuts.

"He loves *kadalakai* [peanuts], my son," says Sarala, with the same tinge of pride with which she talks about her cows and the Alsatian dog that she has kept and now loves. "Whenever he sees peanuts, he won't let them go without stopping and buying some." She has the gift of making commonplace actions sound like achievements. The "Hindi people" and their discriminating palates for her cows' milk, the Alsatian dog's ability to bark for its milk, her son's talent for spotting the fruit carts and peanut vendors with the best products from a mile away—Sarala admires them all. She is an optimist by nature.

On the ride back, I discuss the plan of action with Selva.

"I'll call around and see if anyone has any cows for sale," he says. "Shall we go again tomorrow?"

I nod. The lad is learning. He has at least given me a day's notice.

Over the next few days, we travel to different spots all over the city, either with Kuppa or with their other rickshaw-driver friends to look for a cow. Near Majestic, a crowded neighborhood in the city center named after a movie theater, an entire concrete house has been given up to cows. We peer through the locked grill to see over a dozen cows sitting on the ground with a drain in the middle. A fan whirs above them.

"See how comfortable the owner has made them," says Sarala admiringly. "Only if they are in this comfort will they give good milk."

We visit numerous dwellings like this. They look like people's homes from the outside but are, in fact, homes for cows. In some instances, the family lives on the second floor while the ground floor is for the animals. In others, the family lives in a thatched hut nearby while the government-allotted "low income group" housing unit is given to the cows.

Ram has told me a story about waking up from the dregs of sleep and experiencing a cow sighting in a house like this. When he was about twelve or thirteen, his family home adjoined a slum development with ramshackle huts. During one election cycle, the government upgraded these huts into concrete homes. One morning, Ram woke up, looked out of the window, and stared at the black head of a cow. Actually two. He blinked. The cow mooed in acknowledgement. Or so Ram thought. It was really calling for its owner to come hither and milk. The dairy farmer, who had previously tied his cows outside his hut, had hustled two of his black cows up a flight of stairs and housed them in his government-allotted, one-room house, with the ceiling fan going full blast. There was hay and feed for the animals. The farmer's wife found it easier to scoop up their dung from a cement floor, with a rake and bucket. The farmer put his animals in the apartment allotted to him, and lived outside in a makeshift hut beside the gutter. Everyone in the slum understood; no one complained to the authorities. The whole thing made perfect sense. You did what was best to increase your livelihood.

TYPICALLY WHEN WE SHOW up at a home housing cows, Selva calls the owner, who ambles over from a few houses away. He takes out the cow that is on the market, and Selva walks the cow around, despite the whizzing motorbikes everywhere. Most of the city cows are priced at thirteen hundred dollars and at the end of ten minutes, we tell the owner that his price doesn't "set" for us and take our leave.

After a couple of days of this, Selva and I are both dispirited. Sarala blames our failure on the planets. "I told you that we should have looked for a good day to start this project."

Indians have a concept called Rahu Kalam, or the "Time of Planet Rahu," which is considered to be a bad time to begin things. The time of Rahu is memorized through a silly mnemonic: "Mother Saw Father Wearing The Turban Suddenly." Each time slot is an hour and a half, with the clock beginning at 7:30 a.m. So the bad time on Monday (Mother) would be 7:30 to 9:00, the next would be Saturday (Saw) at 9:00 to 10:30, and so on.

I grew up in a family in which omens were respected, though I have mostly disregarded them since adulthood. My grandparents wouldn't undertake a journey without considering the *shagunam* (signs), also called *nimitta*. It was a three-step process. First they would make sure that the day was good. Then they would choose a time that was not within the Rahu Kalam. Finally, just before setting out, they would look for omens. If a dog scratched its ear as they stepped out, they would come back and sit down for a few minutes, because it indicated failure in the venture. Typically, the cure for such inauspicious omens at the time of departure was to come back and sit down for a few minutes and maybe drink a glass of water. Then you could start again.

As children, we were not allowed to ask the question we most wanted to ask when the grown-ups got ready to leave. "Where are you going?" brought on bad luck as well as clips on our ears. Sneezing, too, was a bad sign and meant that you couldn't leave right away. Crows cawing meant that unexpected guests were on the way. Conversely, if unexpected guests came, they were greeted with, "It's going to rain today because you have come." Hearing the song of a koel was good but seeing one was not. Black crows were a reminder of our ancestors and were fed rice balls and black sesame seeds. The sound of a lizard signaled prosperity.

One omen that I have come to detest involves women: sighting a married woman brings about good luck, while sighting a widow is unlucky. As do some other Hindu rituals, this one seems blatantly sexist to me, for no such rule exists for widowers.

Sarala believes in omens and rituals. So in deference to her, we decide to make our next trip on a day of her choosing.

16

THE CATTLE FAIR

IT IS BEFORE DAWN when we leave home. Sarala and I are on our way to a weekly *santhe* (cattle fair), an all-day affair where thousands of cows, bulls, and calves are bought and sold. Selva and I have had a huge fight—well, in a manner of speaking.

Why don't we visit two or three cattle markets and get a lay of the land before buying a cow, I tell him, particularly since the last few trips have been such debacles.

He cannot take time off from work, he says.

He is willing to spend a ton of money on a cow but cannot exercise due diligence on his investment. I think he would waste less time in the long run if he researched up front.

Why don't you call your friends and see if a cow is available instead of just showing up? I ask.

Because a cow is available one day and sold the next. It is not like bottled water, where Senthil has a large inventory, Selva replies.

I decide to fly solo. I enlist his mother as co-pilot. We are going to check out a cattle fair by ourselves. Surprisingly, even Sarala hasn't gone to many of these. She says that it is a man's job to buy cows. They won't take women seriously. Her tone implies that they definitely won't take me seriously. So I play the trump card. I tell Sarala that there is a famous temple that I want to visit. A tribal goddess who will grant all wishes. Sarala, I know, wants another grandchild. She wants her remaining three sons to get married. She wants more calves from her cows, more milk. She needs a wish-granting goddess like no one else. The cattle market is a sideshow as far as she is concerned.

Selva doesn't even look up from his milking when I tell him that I plan to go to a cattle market that day.

"If you see an animal you like, just buy it," he mutters.

"He is upset because one of the cows is sick and the vet is demanding lots of money for injections," Sarala explains. "This is why we need to keep desi cows. They won't fall as sick."

That's neither here nor there. They may hark after native breeds, but in the end, they buy HF cows for the milk.

With Selva's blessing, such as it is, we set off.

Every village in India seems to have a santhe. The big ones are in North India: Sonepur Cattle Fair in Bihar, where a vast number of cows, and a few elephants, camels, and horses are bought and sold; and in Rajasthan, the famous ones are at Pushkar, Nagaur, Jhalawar, Gangapur, and Kolayat, where camels and cattle are traded with gusto and a measure of trust.

Sarala and I aren't going to any of those. Our destination is much more modest. It is the cattle fair in Dindigul district in the South Indian state of Tamil Nadu. This is Sarala's idea. I don't speak good Kannada (the language of Karnataka state, of which Bangalore is the capital). Speaking the local language is crucial for negotiation. I do speak fluent Tamil. Why not go to a cattle market in Tamil Nadu? says Sarala. After all, it is only three or four hours away.

I pick up Sarala at 5 a.m. and we are on our way. She and I look like sisters. I have jasmine strings in my hair and a round, red *bindi* on my forehead. I am clad in a traditional cotton sari. Wearing anything else will make me stand out as a "modern Madam" and will hike up the price of the cow that I may want to buy.

Sarala is a very pleasant companion. She knows when to keep quiet and when to talk. I know she has rarely been out alone with an unrelated lady in a car. When Sarala travels, it is en famille, in a bus or other public transport, and only after a great deal of planning and collecting stuff—food, clothes, and trinkets—as gifts for whomever she is going to visit. Taking off on a lark for a day is something that she has never done, she says.

Plus, she doesn't know how to buy a cow, she insists. But I have a secret weapon. I am meeting an expert. His name is Johnson Dandapani and I have found him through a twisting ribbon of online connections, all of whom share a love for the cow. "India's religion is not Hinduism; it is *Bos indicus*," writes one of them.

We see many species of *Bos indicus* as we drive through the winding roads. Sarala points them out like Ram points out cars on American highways.

"Oh, wow, look at that black Konga cow," says Sarala. "Its horns alone will make it a prize cow."

"We just passed an Ongole bull," she says later. "I haven't seen those in years."

"That is a Malai Konga cow. Reared by tribal Todas on top of the Blue Mountains. Their milk is like nectar."

Dust flies behind my small car as we turn onto smaller and smaller roads. Boys playing with tires jump up when they see me on the country roads. "Hey, look. A woman is driving the car," shouts one as they all run beside the car.

Our first stop is Sathyamangalam, where Sarala has family. It is a small village in Tamil Nadu, known for its *Boom Boom maadu* (Boom Boom cow), which can predict the future. The last trip was a failure, Sarala says, because we didn't get proper blessings, didn't check omens. This time, she wants to get the blessing from a cow to buy another of its species. A particular group of tribal people ply this trade.

Sarala and I pull up in front of her relative's hut just as the sun rises. It is 7 a.m. There is a welcome committee waiting for us. They offer us *kanji*, which is chilled porridge made with millets, buttermilk, chopped onion, green chilies, and salt. As we eat outside, we hear the sound of cowbells. Along comes a gaily festooned cow on a long leash held by a tribal cowherd. The cow has a pink blanket on its back and a trail of bells around its neck and all over its back—draped like Christmas lights on a tree. Its horns are capped with bells and its hooves have anklets.

Sarala has brought offerings for the cow that can predict the future. She holds out a plate of sugarcane, coconut, beaten and sweetened rice, jaggery, some lentils, groundnut, and hay. The man stands in front of Sarala and me and addresses us in a singsong voice. "Thanks to the Lord of the Seven Hills, we are here to give some good news to this wonderful couple—actually two women, but they are like our mothers. They are like cows, which also are our mothers. And what would you wish to say to these two cow-mothers? Do you have good news for them?"

The cow nods its head. Boom boom, clang the bells.

"Will their families be healthy and prosperous?"

Boom boom. The cow nods its head.

"Will the activity that brings them to our village be successful?"

Again, the cow nods vigorously.

"Okay, since you have given them good tidings, why don't you honor them with a bow."

The cow bends on its ankles like a circus elephant and bows its head.

Sarala is beaming. "When I was a girl, we never used to start on an enterprise before getting the blessing of the Boom Boom cow and a parrot that could tell the future," she says. She offers the plate of goodies to the cowherd, who scoops them all up in the yellow, hand-stitched bag that he is carrying. I slip a couple of bills in the bag as well and off they go. We hear the bells long after they disappear from sight.

Now Sarala is ready for the market.

It is hard to miss a cattle fair. Everyone in the village is heading to it that morning. Men leading cows; cows leading men . . . well, that's pretty much it. We reach an open ground with cows as far as the eye can see: gray, black, and white bovines that stand placidly in the receding mist, waving their tails to swat flies and stamping their feet every now and then. There are trees in the middle and makeshift tea stalls in some corners.

Sarala and I go to a tea stall and wonder how we are going to find my cow adviser, Johnson, in this sea of men. As it turns out, he finds us. Women are few and far between at a cattle fair.

"Shoba Madam?" says a voice. I turn and find a young man, probably in his twenties, thin and gangly, with skin the color of midnight and eyes that shine. He looks both tentative and tough, if that is possible. He is wearing a white dhoti and a matching starched, white shirt.

He smiles uncertainly, glancing at both of us. Sarala is in a good mood. She is chewing peanuts and nods at the young man expansively. He politely asks if we had a comfortable journey and offers to buy us some tea. He works in a call center and has taken time off to come and meet us.

Shouldn't we rush into the market before all the best cows get sold? I ask.

Neither Sarala nor Johnson is in a rush. They savor the tea and the morning sunshine. They are relaxed and cheerful. Life's little moments to be enjoyed. I force my whirring brain to slow down and take a few deep breaths. No hurry, I tell myself. Be in the moment. We are just exploring.

Sarala and Johnson have exchanged their family trees and already discovered mutual friends. Johnson says that he is a "converted Christian." His parents are Hindu but he converted to Christianity because he wanted to join the army. People told him that Christians were needed to fill a quota and he would get in more easily. Turned out he didn't pass the physical exam because he had a hole in his heart. By then it was too late. "I had become a Christian," he says. "Too much work to reconvert back into Hinduism."

We finish our tea and wade into the market. I pick my way behind Johnson, ignoring the curious stares from the men all around.

"What kind of cow do you want to buy?" he asks.

"I am not sure. A good milker?"

I look at Sarala for cues but she is reveling in being amidst the cows. She strokes the back of one as she passes by, touches the forehead of another, pats a third, and nuzzles a fourth.

Johnson says, "Buying a cow is like entering a marriage. A cow that is good for me may not be good for you. Can you marry my wife?"

Over the next hour, we examine several Indian cows, each with a hump on its back. "*Go purathaha iti go-puram*," says Johnson in Sanskrit. "Because of this raised hump, the temple structure is called *go-puram*." All Hindu temples have a raised go-puram (pyramid-like structure) like the spire of a church. The larger ones have it on four sides. I hadn't realized that the name for this architectural element was borrowed from the cow (*go*). I wish those composting kids were here with me. Imagine that, I would tell them. Yet another thing—this time an Indian architectural icon—originating from a bovine icon.

Sometimes the cow's hump is a little off center. That is not good. An imbalanced hump leads to an imbalanced cow. Then there is the dewlap that hangs from below the neck. In a bull, the dewlap should not hang lower than the "sheath" or the underbelly. A hanging dewlap in a bull is a symbol of infertility, says Johnson. But we are not in the market for a bull so it really doesn't matter.

The most important thing to check is the whorls that appear on different parts of the cow. Johnson points at the cow that has a whorl—where the fur grows in the opposite of the usual direction. "If there is an umbrella-shaped whorl on the umbrella-shaped forehead of the cow, it can give good things to one person, or one blow after another for another person," says Johnson. It sounds more musical in Tamil.

He describes a cow that his family bought with just such a whorl. "The cow brought so much good luck for me. I had a business selling turmeric and my business boomed after the cow arrived. It brought bad luck for my father, on the other hand. His wells went dry after the cow arrived and so his farm gave less paddy. Same family. Same cow. Different outcomes."

After they sold the cow, the opposite happened. Johnson's turmeric business collapsed but his father's water situation improved.

"So what do you do? Try out the cow to see if it brings you luck?" I ask jokingly.

To my surprise, Johnson nods. "That's how it used to be done in the old days," he says. "Anytime you bought a valuable object, be it a diamond or a cow, you'd keep it at home for a few days to see what effect it had on your family. If it brought bad luck, you could return the cow, no questions asked. Because the same cow could bring good luck to another family."

"What is called 'right fit' in the corporate world," I murmur.

Sarala tells me about whorls on the underbelly of the cow. Johnson's expertise has made her insecure. She feels that she has to prove herself.

"Lots of people use whorls as a reason to discard cows. I am not one of those," she says, frowning disapprovingly at Johnson as if he were one of those offenders. "Whorls are like a dish antenna, or a blueprint. They tell you a lot about the nervous system and energy flow in the animal."

"Yes, *Akka*. You are so right," says Johnson, endearing himself to her by calling her "Akka" (elder sister) and massaging her ego. "The trick is to match the animal's energy and temperament to yours. For example, if you are a rough and tough sort, you can buy an animal with a double whorl in the flank. This means that the cow is high-spirited; it has a dual personality. Needs to be handled with care."

"In my family, we never buy animals with double whorls—two whorls on the same side of the flank," says Sarala. "Better to have one whorl on one flank and the other on the other flank. That means that the whorls are equally balanced on both sides. Then, that animal will be well-balanced, passive. Even an old person like my husband can handle such a cow."

Johnson nods vigorously. "The trick is to choose the animal based on your capabilities, not the animal's capabilities."

This time, Sarala nods agreement. They all nod, even the cows.

Actually, though these theories sound a little crazy, hair whorls have long fascinated horse and cattle breeders, as well as animal scientists, who have linked them to temperament. Dr. Temple Grandin, the author of *Animals in Translation*, showed a connection between "high whorls" above the animal's forehead and an excitable temperament. On her website, she uses horses as examples to prove her points, but I guess the same could apply to cows.

As we slowly pick our way through the animals, I am drawn to a red cow with its calf nearby. Its owner watches as the three of us walk around the animal. Diagonally opposite the urethra is a whorl. "This is called a water swirl," says Johnson. He takes some mud and rubs it on the swirl. Immediately, the animal starts urinating.

He quickly walks away from the animal. Sarala and I follow him. "People will usually avoid buying a cow with a water swirl," he says. "They may give you good milk but they are high maintenance. They have a loose urethra. Incontinence."

Sarala adds, "They are high-strung animals and require a lot of love and affection. The only time when people will buy these types of animals is when they have more than six cows so that their temperaments balance each other. They will get affection and sympathy from each other. I have one such cow in my herd. The other cows have calmed her down."

I cannot take my eyes away from the red cow. She is a beautiful animal with an arched forehead, hanging ears, lots of skin under her neck (the dewlaps), and eyes the size of oval macaroons. She likes me, too. I can tell by the way her eyes follow me. She has an air of utter trust and stillness—it calms me down yet quickens my pulse.

"How much is he asking for it?"

Johnson whips out a towel, throws it over his hand. This is a signal. The owner clasps Johnson's hand. Sarala tells me that it is all a matter of clasping the hand and pressing. If you press one time, it means that you are offering a particular amount that varies from market to market. It could mean a thousand or ten thousand rupees.

"This is why women don't come to the santhe," says Sarala. "Which man will take a woman's hand under the towel and start pressing her palm? The woman's husband will cut off the other man's hand."

Johnson pulls us aside after the negotiation. He tells us that he has pressed six times—for an offer price of sixty thousand rupees.

"But I didn't tell you to make an offer!" I say. "I just wanted to know the price."

"Oh really? *Iyyo.*" Tamil for "Oh, dear." Johnson stares at me uncertainly.

"Tell him that you pressed his hand by accident."

"You can't. When you are negotiating under the towel, your word is the law."

Or the press of the hand is the law.

Thankfully for us, the seller wants eighty thousand for the cow. It is a young heifer, he says. A virgin cow that hasn't calved. After two calves, the heifer will be called a cow.

The lack of a contract or any other legal paper has made me both rash and confident. "What happens if we agree on a price but don't take the cow?" I ask.

Sarala stares at me horrified. "They will beat us up and not let us leave this place without paying the money," she replies simply.

"How do you bring the price down to fifty thousand?" I ask.

"I can't. I have already offered sixty K," Johnson hisses in colloquial Tamil, staring at me.

We are all at cross-purposes. Both Sarala and Johnson don't understand what I am doing. To be fair, I am not sure what I am doing either.

"Why do you want this incontinent cow, Madam?" asks Sarala.

"Do you think it will give good milk?" I ask in return.

Sarala nods. The milk quality is not the problem.

"Why do you care about incontinence?" I push. "After all, it is not as if the animal lives on a carpet and you have to clean up the

urine each time. Just let it drain out of the cowshed. Or sell the
urine. Isn't it better if you touch her back and she urinates? You
can have a bottle at the ready."

Sarala smiles. "I see now what is happening. You have fallen in
love with this animal. That happened to me all the time. Okay, let
us see if she is destined to be yours."

Johnson smiles. He, too, gets it now.

I am not sure if I have fallen in love with the red cow. But I really want to bid for this animal. I am confident that the seller won't
lower the price. I want to see how this plays out. I have back-up
plans and rationalizations. If by chance the seller does cave, I am
stuck with a cow, albeit one that we got at a good price. Or we can
simply leave town without paying. In my mind, all these are possible scenarios.

Johnson walks back to the man. There is a small group of turbaned men who are watching us. Probably placing bets on whether
these city slickers will get the cow or be outsmarted by one of
them, I think sourly.

Sarala tries to explain how the smaller negotiations happen,
though she isn't completely certain, having never done it before.
"If you press his thumb alone, you are asking for a 10 percent discount. If you press the index finger, 20 percent discount. And so
it goes," she says.

We watch the two men, a towel over their hands, their eyes
locked on each other but otherwise motionless.

Johnson walks back to us, shaking his head. I open my mouth
but Sarala shushes me into silence. The code of the market is that
the actual prices aren't talked about aloud. Nobody needs to know

each cow's price except the buyer and the seller, she says. That is the whole point of covering your hands with a towel.

"Cows are like humans. Each cow is different. That's why each animal has a unique price," she says. "Discussing the cow's price in public is disrespectful. Would you discuss your daughter's price in public? Even if you had to get her married off and give her a dowry?"

I don't get the analogy but am not really listening. The red cow is looking at me. She is mine. I know it. If Selva doesn't like this cow, I'll just buy him another. That's how mesmerized I am by this cow. I'm no longer being rational.

"How did it go?" I ask Johnson. "Did he bring down the price even a little?"

The seller is firm, says Johnson. We have several things against us. First of all, these men aren't taking us seriously, he says.

When I ask why, he hesitates.

"Because we are women." Sarala has an answer. "From the city. Why would they trust us?"

But there is more, Johnson tells us. The real reason for his stubbornness is that he doesn't want to sell his cow to us city folks who live far away.

Sarala understands. "Madam, you are a mother," she says. "If you had a choice between marrying off your daughter to someone from the next town and someone from North India, wouldn't you choose the man close by? So that you can at least go and visit your girl once in a month. The same with this cow. The seller may not have the money to maintain her but he wants to see her, make sure she is okay. If he sells to us and we take her to Bangalore, he knows that he will never see his cow again. Why would he do that?"

At that moment, I realize that we are wasting our time. Nobody in this cattle market will sell to us, no matter what the price. It turns out to be true. We walk around for a few hours. With every cow, I increase my offer price, knowing that I am being reckless yet unable to stop myself. Johnson negotiates for various cows, even the ones he doesn't recommend because they have whorls indicating personalities that won't suit mine.

How do you know my personality? I ask.

Again he hesitates. "City people are used to getting their way," he says. "They think that money can buy anything. Mostly it can. But not a cow. This black cow that you were willing to pay ninety thousand rupees for is equally strong-minded. Look at this whorl on one side of its neck. That shows stubbornness. If I saddle you with an opinionated cow . . . "

He and Sarala look at each other and laugh.

"It will result in a volcano," she says.

"The cow is for Sarala," I say. "And anyway I am not stubborn. I am actually very soft and flexible. I can manage a cow with any personality. You should meet my family . . . They are all so headstrong and I get along with them . . . "

Sarala and Johnson have walked on.

The sun gets higher and the earth gets hotter. Around noon, Sarala and I walk out of the market with no cow. As soon as I get into the car, I take a deep breath and feel the rush of bidding for animals drain away from me. Is this how auctions work? People walk in with no intention of buying anything and yet can't stop themselves from raising the paddle higher and higher? What was I thinking? Thank God the sellers were more sensible than me.

"We didn't go to that temple," says Sarala, trying to console me. "That is why we didn't get the red cow."

"But we did visit the Boom Boom cow first," I reply, even though I am not sure I need consolation. I feel strange, wobbly. It's like a crash after a sugar high.

"So what about the good-luck temple that you told me about?"

I feel ashamed for lying to her. I consider whether I should lie some more and take her to some random temple in the area. After all, Indian villages are full of temples.

I tell her the truth. I apologize. I tell her that I will pray that she gets another grandchild, a girl this time.

Sarala nods. I cannot tell if she is mad at me or just hungry like I am.

Johnson takes us to his simple but gorgeous mud house. There are white drawings on the walls. Fifteen cows graze in the back field. Red chilies are spread out on the verandah in front to sundry. Johnson's mother makes us a simple lunch of hot red rice with some gravy—it looks like *sambhar* but I am not really sure. Banana leaves are spread out on the floor. We sit cross-legged while Johnson's mother serves. Hot red rice, some ghee, and a gravy. Heavenly.

A FEW HOURS LATER, Sarala and I take our leave. We don't talk much in the car. Sarala naps. It is evening by the time we hit the outskirts of Bangalore.

"Let's have some tea in my cousin's house, Madam," says Sarala.

We turn off the highway once more and drive down winding country roads. The sun is setting. Dusk is a magical time in Indian villages. The heat of the day recedes and a pleasant chill settles like a blanket. It is the time when mother cows rush home to be with their calves. I told the kids about it during the composting lesson. It's when the dust from their hooves, called *go-dhuli* (cow dust), rises up and creates a phantasmagorical landscape. Women stack cow-dung patties into a pyramid-shaped mound and set fire to them. Smoke rises like tendrils. A reddish hue spreads across the sky as the sun sets.

Go-dhuli bela means cow-dust time. *Go* is cow, *dhuli* is dust, and *bela* is time. According to Sanskrit scholar Bibek Debroy this is "a very Bengali expression." Debroy, with whom I communicate through email, is the author of an unabridged translation of the *Mahabharata* epic. "The three *sandhyas* [dawn, noon, dusk] are auspicious and important, especially dawn and dusk, because they represent 'joins' in divisions of the day. It also happens to be the time that the cows come home."

These "joins" are important in Hinduism because they signify the hours when the gods come out to play. There are songs, shows, and movies that center around cow-dust time. The most famous Indian film about it is by Girish Karnad and B. V. Karanth, who belong to my home state of Karnataka, in South India. In 1977, they made a Hindi film called *Godhuli*, based on a short story by Munshi Premchand. The much-lauded film is about what cows mean to a family and village. The film opens with the village head-man's son, Nandan, who has returned to India with his American wife, Lydia. Young Nandan wants to reform the village. He views cows merely as dairy products rather than symbols central to the rural milieu. (It's not unlike my cousin Vic's disdain for the cow rituals his father insisted on in his new apartment.)

Nandan starts a dairy business with modern farming techniques. When a cow stops producing, he sends the aging cow to the slaughterhouse. Hearing this, the incensed village priest curses the entire family. Your clan will come to an end because you are sending a cow to her death, he says. Nandan's mother donates cows to the village priest to appease him, so that he will retract his curse. Lydia becomes pregnant. Does the American wife deliver a baby? Is the baby's life threatened? Does the cow die? Does the young man win over the village or does he pack up and return to America? Well, you'll have to watch the film to see.

North Indians celebrate weddings and engagements during cow-dust time. In South India, though, it is viewed a little more cautiously. For my cousins and me, Vic included, walking back exhausted from swimming and playing at the river, this cow-dust time was when our mothers called us inside. Evil spirits were freed from the trees under the cloak of the descending darkness, they said. Better to stay indoors. We children would wash our feet, apply sacred ash (also made from cow dung, by the way), on our foreheads, say our prayers in front of the family *puja* altar, and get down to the hated chore of homework.

Sarala and I witness this magical cow-dust time as we drive to her cousin's house. Smoke snakes out of small village bonfires. Dust is stirred up by the feet of herds running home. The sun casts an orange haze over the landscape. We drink some tea, wait for the dust to settle and the sun to set, and slowly make our way back home.

17

BUYING A COW

A WEEK LATER, SELVA has some news. "Reddy has a cow," he tells his mother. Reddy is a man who sold them a cow in the past. When Selva called three weeks ago, Reddy told Selva that he had no cows for sale. Apparently that has changed. So we go to visit Reddy.

Varthur village lies beyond the gated communities just outside Bangalore. Kuppa is driving. Today Sarala's elder son, Senthil, is also with us. He rides shotgun, hopping off at every traffic signal to avoid getting fined by cops. We get into a skirmish because a red Honda Accord bangs into our rickshaw. Kuppa and the two boys leap out to argue with the errant driver. After an hour of discussion, the man pays them five dollars. Sarala and I sit in the rickshaw, chewing on peanuts and discussing our lives.

We have wasted an hour for five bucks, I think but don't say.

Vegetable vendors line the entrance to Varthur village with fresh greens, tomatoes, and the rest of the day's harvest piled in stacks. We stop to buy some vegetables for our homes, place them in the back of the rickshaw before carrying on.

Rajashekar Reddy is tall and imposing, with the deliberate gait of age and encumbrances. He welcomes us with the cordiality of a man who is about to see good money, and takes us to his cows. There are four of them in the paddock, feeding on hay. As always, Sarala is all admiration—for the cows, the setting, and Reddy. Her husband is not with her so she can be free with her compliments.

"See how strong he is," she nods towards Reddy. "Drinking fresh milk daily, breathing this eucalyptus-scented air, eating home-grown vegetables harvested from this red earth. What's not to like about this life?"

In her voice, I hear longing. She has told me that Selva dreams of returning to Arni, their native village, buying a few cows and a small plot of land, and living a life that Reddy seems to enjoy now. The only problem is that they have a lot of debts and until those are repaid, they are tied to the city.

Selva and Senthil examine the four cows in the paddock. The animals grunt and stamp when the boys approach them. "Hey, hey," they say, quieting the cows. They open the mouth of one cow, smell its saliva, lift its tail, peer into its rectum, and look at the legs for sores or wounds.

Reddy shows us the calf, which has apparently been raised on bucket milk. We learn that it was not fed from its mother's udder.

"That's not good," Sarala whispers to me. "Just to save your-self the work of untying the calf every morning and then leading it back from its mother after it feeds, these people have taken a

shortcut. Shouldn't the calf experience the pleasure of drinking milk from its mother? Doesn't the cow deserve to honor its maternity by feeding its young? Bad for the mother; bad for the calf."

The two boys choose one of Reddy's cows. Like all these cows, it is a Holstein-Friesian with black and white markings. I can't see any difference from the other three. It looks healthy, well fed, and amiable. When I walk close to it, the cow glances at me from the corner of its eye but remains unconcerned.

Reddy wants $1200 for it and does not want to bargain. He bought it for $1300 a couple of years ago, he says. It is a good milker, giving about seventeen liters of milk per day. By now, I am getting used to this urban myth that Bangalore cows give seventeen liters of milk a day—no more, no less. Everyone quotes seventeen.

Selva comes to me and says that it will be hard to beat this deal. "You saw how it is," he says. "People won't reduce their price just like that."

I ask Reddy if he will take $1000. That's all the money I have with me, I say. We go back and forth for a while. Our language is flowery, yet laced with insults.

"I am getting the good fortune of buying a cow for the first time. Why don't you let me have that good karma by lowering your price?" I ask Reddy. "Why must you fleece me?"

"It is my honor that a lady from a big apartment complex has come to buy my cow," replies Reddy. "Why would I cheat you? I want more business people who read computers like you. Only if you patronize cows will this country succeed."

I don't see the connection between cows and this country's success, but I let it go.

"Reduce the price by $200 and make it $1000 even," I say, coming straight to the point, like these people do.

"No can do, Madam," replies Reddy. "This is a good cow. Its milk will taste like ambrosia. Drink it and you are set for life. But then, what will you computer people know about the value of a good cow?"

Selva speaks Kannada and he steps in. The men get down to business. The negotiation concludes in minutes. "He won't come down below $1100," says Selva.

"I don't have that much," I reply, pulling out the $1000.

"It's all right," says Selva. "Pay him what you have and we can take him the rest tomorrow."

Reddy brings out a brass plate with betel leaves, betel nuts, a broken coconut, and a few bananas—all symbols of fertility and prosperity—for our new cow. She has a stillness about her that is both reassuring and eerie. All cows are contemplative. Our cow is positively Zen. Selva, Sarala, and I stand on one side, holding the brass plate and laying our cash on it. Reddy and his cow stand on the other. Senthil takes photos on his mobile phone. The deal is concluded.

Reddy ceremoniously leads us to his house—a one-room dwelling, sparsely furnished, with electric-blue walls and a black, concrete floor. We sit on chairs. Reddy's daughter-in-law brings out hot milk, tea, biscuits, peanuts, and savory snacks. Reddy urges us to eat. Sarala does her eyebrow-raised, half-smile expression of admiration.

"Now that he has our money, he can afford to be generous," she mumbles.

We chew on peanuts and exchange gossip about cows. Reddy tells us that the cow we are buying has a good temperament. "She won't run; she won't hit you with her horns. She is a family-oriented cow."

A little while later, the van arrives. The men bring a wooden plank, angle it against the van, stand behind the cow and push. After resisting a bit, the surprised cow scoots up the plank and into the van. Kuppa has left with the rickshaw, so we can ride back together with our cow to Bangalore: humans in front and the cow in the back. The trip costs ten dollars. I run up to my apartment and come back down to the van to give Selva and Sarala the remaining money for the cow.

"Why don't you buy us the first feed? That will give you some extra good fortune," suggests Sarala.

We go to a shop very near my house and buy cow feed. The typical ratio is crushed whole maize (30 percent), cottonseed-extract cakes (20 percent), milled legumes like horse gram, soy, black-eyed peas (15 percent), milled wheat (15 percent), and salt, mineral, and vitamin mix for the remainder. It comes to one hundred fifty dollars.

The van deposits us outside Sarala's cowshed at the end of my road. Its location, right beside the milk parlor and the drain, allows for outlets for all of the cow's secretions. Sarala and her family toss the cow dung into the drain and sell leftover milk to the Nandini milk booth. After the van leaves, Sarala asks me to hold the reins, and with great solemnity we walk our cow into her new home: a thatched-roof cowshed with a dirt floor.

"Name her, Madam," says Sarala.

Here? I think, looking at the cow dung on the floor, the stink of

the drain nearby and the three other cows staring at me. What did I expect? The White House? Sarala and her boys are in a hurry. They have to return to work. Selva has to bathe the cows; Senthil has to go deliver water; Sarala needs to go home to cook for her family.

They tell me to come up with a name and whisper it into the cow's ear three times. The name has to end with *Lakshmi*. Otherwise the name won't set, says Sarala.

Okay, I say, let's call her Raja Lakshmi. Royal Lakshmi.

That's taken.

What about Dhana Lakshmi—Prosperous Lakshmi? Taken, too. Gaja Lakshmi—Elephant-venerating Lakshmi? Taken. All the eight traditional Lakshmi (Ashta Lakshmi) names—Brave Lakshmi, Child-holding Lakshmi, Brilliant Lakshmi—are already taken by Sarala's herd.

It can end with *Gowri*, too, says Sarala, as a compromise.

I tell her that I will think about it. Let us choose a good day for this important undertaking, I hedge.

AT HOME, I SUDDENLY discover that I have lots of friends. "My daughter has bought a cow," my mom tells her siblings, cousins, aunts, and uncles excitedly. Everyone has suggestions about names. My kids want to name the cow Laika, after the first dog that orbited space.

But it is a cow, not a dog, I say.

No matter, it is an animal, they reply.

"Will Laika-Lakshmi work?" I ask Sarala.

"Laika sounds like the name of a detergent powder," she replies.

My uncle wants me to name the cow after my great-grandmother, Seshambal, but Seshambal Lakshmi is too verbose.

My husband wants to name the cow after his sister. It will be both an act honoring his sister and the gleefully teasing act of a younger brother. I think it would be cool to have a cow named after me, but I want to make sure my sister-in-law is okay with it.

I call her in the United States and ask permission. Sure, she says.

"How about Anantha Lakshmi?" I ask Sarala the next day. "Is that taken, too?"

She ponders. I wonder why. "Okay," she says finally. "Let's call her Anantha Lakshmi." Blissful-Lakshmi.

I like it.

I take a deep breath and bend over to whisper the name three times into the cow's wide black ear.

"You are Anantha Lakshmi," I say. "Anantha Lakshmi is your name. Anantha Lakshmi."

The cow twitches her ear and listens.

Months later, during our regular, desultory morning conversation, I ask Sarala for the name of the cow that got hit by a corporation truck.

"What was the name of the cow that got hit?" I ask.

"Her name was Anantha-Lakshmi," says Sarala. "Same name as your cow."

"Actually, it will soon be your cow," I finally tell her. "My family and I plan to donate the cow to you for my father and father-in-law's eightieth birthday."

Sarala beams. "You are doing a good thing, Madam," she says. "It will bring good luck to the family. Nothing higher than a cow donation."

Both birthdays are still a few months away. So, technically, I am at least temporarily the owner of a cow.

HAVE YOU EVER OWNED a cow? It is quite wonderful. I can say this, of course, because I am not doing the dirty work. I have subcontracted the cow's entire care to Sarala and her family. My family does only the fun parts. My kids accompany me across the street with gusto these days. They want to pet the cow. They bring their friends. All the Japanese kids in our building are fascinated by the cow, but they cannot pronounce her name. So everybody has taken to calling her "AL"—short for Anantha Lakshmi.

AL is patient. She doesn't stomp, shake her horns, or swat the kids with her tail. Beyond paying for AL's monthly feed and collecting the milk every day, though, I am distracted, preoccupied elsewhere. Our dog, Inji, has fallen sick. We take her to the vet, Dr. Morton, who tells us that she has a kidney problem. Sarala gives me advice about how to make Inji feel better. She tells me to feed the dog cow urine every day. Inji will not go near it. She detests cows. My Labrador is getting sicker every day and there is nothing I can do about it.

Sarala is preoccupied, too. She wants AL to get pregnant but she wants to make sure that the calf is female. Male cows don't give milk. Bulls are good if you have a field to plough, Sarala tells me. In the dairy community, male calves aren't valued, a contrast to the rest of Indian society, where female infanticide is still a problem.

"There is a new technology, Madam," Sarala says one day. "It can separate the bull semen so that we can get a female calf—guaranteed. Why don't you look into it?"

That evening, Ram and I take our dog to Dr. Morton again. She has been shivering with spasms and has stopped eating. It is the fifth time in two weeks that we are at the vet. After examining her, Dr. Morton sits us down. With kind eyes, he explains that we may have to do kidney dialysis. And even then, he cannot be sure that they can save her.

My husband and I gape at the doctor. What is he saying?

Inji is just three years old. She is a healthy, happy Labrador who likes to eat, not the sort of dog to contract a life-threatening illness. But then, isn't that what all parents—and that is really how I relate to my dog—say when their child succumbs to the lethal march of an illness?

We have many questions. How did she contract it? we ask.

An *E. coli* infection caused the kidney problems. How does anyone contract an infection? asks the doctor in return. We take her for walks outside. She sniffs other dog's shit. (In India, dog owners aren't required to pick up the poop.) There is stagnant water with mosquitoes on the road.

How long does she have to live? Dr. Morton sighs and speaks in generalities. Other dogs have lasted a few months . . .

A few months? That is the outer limit? Ram and I are shocked. Dr. Morton refers us to Cessna Lifeline Veterinary Hospital, with its rotating team of vets. The next month is a whirl. All four of us—Ram, Ranju, Malu, and I—go to the vet every evening. They put Inji on a table and give her IV drips with a cocktail of medicines. She gets weaker. She eats very little. She lies in the sun. When I take her for a walk, she zigzags like a drunk.

Her treatments last an hour each day. We all take turns standing beside Inji as they prod and poke her, hook her up to machines.

When the vets are free, I chat with them. I tell them about Sarala and ask them if there is a way to guarantee a female calf.

One vet, Dr. Chavan, smiles. "Your friend is a dairy farmer, isn't she?" he asks. "There are techniques to guarantee a male calf," he says, "but they are very expensive." He mentions something called "flow cytometry," which sorts the sperm. He gives me the contact number of his friend.

Inji gets worse every day. She goes into surgery for the dog version of dialysis. It doesn't seem to help. I wake up in the morning, dreading the sight of her tired, prone body and feebly wagging tail. I occasionally wish that Inji would die in her sleep (though I am later ashamed to admit that), relieving me of decisions about drugs that don't seem to work, freeing me from days and nights at the clinic. After several weeks of this bleak routine, I just want the whole thing to be over. Not my husband.

People react in different ways to health crises. You learn new things about your spouse and children. Ram, who doesn't even like Inji as much as I do, will not give up on her. He is like a maniac—going on the Internet to discover new medication for chronic kidney failure in dogs. He consults four vets (including one in the United States) about urine cultures and blood reports. That's when our fights begin. We argue over medical protocols and dropping creatinine counts. I want to let Inji finish her life at home, without needles, in peace. He accuses me of pulling the plug, of copping out.

"If one of us has to get cancer, it had better be me because I'll give up on you after a few weeks, just like I am giving up on Inji," I tell him tearfully, because the truth of who I am is now revealed.

"Ask the vet if we should try ciprofloxacin," he replies.

You want to know about grief? Let me tell you about grief—not the spousal grief so beautifully captured by Joan Didion in her book, *The Year of Magical Thinking*. This grief is the kind that is felt by a whole family that watches a beloved pet lose life's last battle. Grief is the sound of IV drips, the coldness of a metal stretcher, and the smell of antiseptic mixed with urine. Grief is a woman spending four hours a day at a vet clinic, watching her once-frisky dog lie still on a metal stretcher and get two bottles of Ringer lactate solution mixed with streptopencillin, B complex, vitamin C, and a cocktail of drugs.

Grief is a husband and wife screaming at each other about appropriate medical procedures. Grief is a man telling his wife, "Why do you have that morose face? Wipe that face off your face. We can still save her. We can change the antibiotic. The creatinine count is still not that low."

Till you experience it, you think that grief is one emotion. It isn't; it is many emotions packaged into one. It's like standing at the top of a tall building and having the floor fall out. There is some of that shock. There is the rage that comes with the "why me" question. There is a bitter taste in your mouth that never seems to go away. There are the questions that sprout up at the oddest moments. Questions like "What is a good way to die?"

SHE HAS BEEN SERIOUSLY sick for five weeks, our dog. Is that too short a time or too long a time to watch her suffer? Is it good that her illness has given our family time to adjust? Or would it have been better if she had suffered a stroke and died the next morning without suffering?

We know the end is nigh.

The night before Inji dies, she and I lie beside each other on the orange couch in our living room. She is too weak to move after a month of not eating. She does not shut her dilated, golden eyes the whole night; neither do I shut mine. I watch my beautiful, beige Labrador, with her still-silky coat, suffer spasms all through the night. The *E. coli* infection that has eaten through her kidneys has finally lodged inside her brain. The shivering that had started six weeks before has turned into violent paroxysms. Let go, child, I whisper to her, as she drools bile and saliva, as her body rattles so hard I hear the emptiness inside. I want her to die; I want the decision not to be mine. Her eyes never leave me, even as I go to get her some water from the kitchen—water that spills from the sides of her mouth. Is she scared? I don't know. I am.

At around 3 a.m. Inji starts frothing at the lips. She has stopped drinking, even water.

The next morning, we take her to the vet. It is over, Dr. Morton says. He has been tracking her since the illness began. Ram and I drive back home with her. We are silent. We follow our usual routine of calling four vets before deciding that the illness has won. My husband, the man who never gives up, finally concedes defeat. He calls my sister-in-law, Priya.

Every family has a different go-to person for different crises. You call your mom for certain things, your dad for others, your siblings for something else. Priya loves all animals and babies. She is the first person we call that evening. She and my brother come over.

We call Dr. Morton and ask him to come. We don't say why and he doesn't ask. When he arrives, we ask if Inji has any chance to recover. He says no. "If I don't anesthetize her now, she'll be dead by tonight. But she'll be in pain the whole day."

We briefly debate whether to pull the kids out of school and end up bringing home our elder daughter, Ranju, now in high school, but leaving Malu, a middle-schooler, out of the whole thing.

At noon, Ranju puts Inji's head on her lap. My mother pours Ganga water into Inji's mouth. My father looks dazed. Everyone weeps.

Our friend, Sriram—a dog lover who simply shows up, as friends do in times of crisis—says, "Watch her eyes. It helps you gain some closure."

So I stare into my dog's eyes, searching for signs of pain or fear. Her eyes remain dilated. Death will occur in a few seconds, says the doctor as he injects her.

In the Vedic period, there was a name for the people who killed the animals used for sacrifices. They were called *samitrs* (quieteners). I read about them in a book called *Violence Denied*, by Jan Houben.

I find myself reflexively whispering things similar to what the samitrs would say to cows before strangling them.

"You are going to live in an auspicious and spacious place, surrounded by nourishing food and drink. You are going to listen to sacred utterances that enhance your spirit. Till the sun shines; till the moon rises; till the ocean has tides; your body and mind will be nourished by love, life, and light. Your fur will exude the fragrance of affection. Your eyes will have the light of someone who has been loved. You are the abode of all the gods. The life of all beings depends on you. Sins will not touch you. Be of good cheer. Go with a peaceful heart. Peace be with you."

I see the light go out of Inji's eyes. With my fingers, I close them. Most of us are sobbing now, bawling. But Ram hasn't shed a tear. That will come later. He has not accepted this yet.

We drive in a motorcade to Kengeri, an hour outside Bangalore, where an organization called People for Animals rescues wildlife that has been cruelly treated by humans and rehabilitates them. They have a pet cemetery on a woody knoll. We bury Inji there with full honors and rites (four pallbearers, sprinkled rice according to Hindu tradition), her favorite foods (milk, bananas) to feed her on her way to the heavens, and a jasmine garland.

Who are you? Are you the kind who grieves intensely and quickly, or does your grief take time to reveal itself and leave? Does it ever leave? As I watch the palpable grief in the people I love, I tell myself that I am different from them, stronger. Not true.

I tell myself I am over it. I say this during those moments when I feel Inji behind me as I boil milk in the kitchen. I say this when I insert the key into my front door and feel my body tighten with pleasure in anticipation of the overjoyed welcome my dog gave me—tail wagging, body shaking from side to side. I still smile when I open the door. And then I stop.

"It has been six months," I tell Sarala. "I miss Inji every day."

She nods sympathetically.

"Animals touch your heart in ways people don't realize," she says. "We have birthed and lost so many cows and calves. It is hard every single time."

18

A CALF

A FEW MONTHS LATER, my cow is pregnant. Sarala announces this one November morning in the matter-of-fact tone that she uses to ask if I want extra milk.

"The cow is pregnant, Madam. Your cow."

I am delighted. Over the next few months, we ply AL with goodies: watermelon rinds, pineapple peels, mango seeds, fresh greens, grains, jaggery water—all of which are to bovines what pop-tarts and pizza are to kids. We want to make AL feel good before her delivery. This is an Indian tradition. Pregnant women, too, are feted and fussed over. No references are made to whales or waddling. Instead, people send over special snacks and handmade delicacies. Feeding a pregnant woman, it is said, assures a seat in heaven.

Sarala and I examine AL every day. Sarala says that the cow's

face has softened, acquired a maternal character. AL gets her special pregnancy food from multiple households in the neighborhood. My kids canvass the neighbors for orange peels and coconut
scrapings. No bones, no meat, no eggshells—nothing nonvegan.
Our cook, Geeta, adds another element. No leftovers that have
touched our lips.

"The cow is a holy animal, Madam," she says.

This notion of contamination by saliva is common in Indian
dining etiquette. Every Indian language has a word for it. In Tamil,
we call it *echal*. In Hindi, they call it *jhoota*, or *geela*. The closest
American approximation is double-dipping, when guests dip their
tortilla chip into the dip again after taking a bite, thus befouling
the dip with their spit, as it were. Think of this to the nth degree,
and you'll get an idea of the Indian concept of impurity through
saliva.

Our cook believes that giving the "pure" cow our saliva-
contaminated leftovers is a sin. She looks through the cow bucket
and vets every discard. Once, I casually threw in a string of jasmine. The flowers had faded but I knew the cow would eat them.
"The string will tie itself around the cow's intestines and may kill
it," said our cook disapprovingly, pulling out the offending string
of jasmine.

The kids and I want to see the cow deliver. We keep telling
Sarala to phone us when it happens. She agrees in theory but cannot guarantee it. "Some cows will deliver at night," she says queru-
lously when we bring up the subject yet again. "Even I won't be
present. They'll undergo all the labor pain and deliver the baby
calf by themselves, poor things."

One morning, after the milking, Sarala leads the pregnant cow

into the army enclave. I follow. Grazing on the fresh grass inside
will relax AL, she says. At around 10:30 a.m. on the following day,
the security guard outside my building phones me. My cow is in
labor, he says.

I race downstairs and see a crowd gathered at the gate of the
army enclave. AL is on the main road inside. I push my way
through to where Sarala, Naidu, and Selva are standing beside AL
with gunnysacks. AL is snorting a bit, blowing mist through her
nostrils. But beyond that, her face is the same. She is not screaming
like human women do in labor. She stands, then sits, then changes
position—to push, I presume. The whole process takes thirty minutes. AL delivers a sprightly, healthy calf right there on the main
road inside a clean army compound.

The calf arrives swathed in membrane. It lies on the ground.
Two minutes later, it lifts up its head. AL licks the calf all over
to remove the protective sheath and clean her. Ten minutes later,
the calf hobbles up. Mother and calf nuzzle and bond. Sarala and
Naidu pour water on the tar road to wash out the blood. They
clean the area with brooms and sprinkle cow-dung water all over.
Finally, they scoop up the newborn calf in the sack and walk the
tired new mother to the cowshed down the road. We all admire
the calf's beautiful white and black markings. There is just one
problem: the calf is male.

Does Sarala view her cows as gifts of nature or as gravy trains?
The answer is both. She juggles both perspectives on a daily, almost minute-to-minute basis. This gift of nature, this calf, as I find
out, is to be gifted away.

Sarala gives the new cow-mother a healing diet for three days.
She mixes cane sugar with grains and cornstalks. The concoction

will cool her uterus and remove the remaining placenta, she says. She sends Selva to a farm two hours outside Bangalore to collect the corn stalks. Sarala thinks that the new mother needs this extra nutrition. As compromises go, it is a small but important one. Sarala doesn't *need* to give the new cow-mother a special diet. It is not as if the cow will demand tasty cornstalks or throw a tantrum (although cows do). Selva would probably prefer not to ride two hours to pay for and bring back piles of prickly cornstalks. Naidu probably will complain about aching joints and extra work because Selva isn't there to pick up the slack. But they do it, not because they need to, not because they even want to, but because . . . they can. It is possible—nobody is sick that day, they aren't short of cash—so they go the extra mile for the cow.

"Does the cow have a mouth to tell you its pain?" asks Sarala. "After all, we are women, too. It is up to us to take care of them."

The affection that Sarala feels for her cattle is genuine and is part of the reason why I find her, and her ecosystem, so compelling. Most urban encounters with nature are fleeting, optional, and impersonal. We go bird watching, visit the zoo, and grow vegetables in the garden. Truly immersive experiences involve living with another species within their natural habitat for long periods of time. Urban dairy farmers allow me to get a glimpse of such a relationship without having to leave the city, or even my neighborhood. They allow me to witness the intersection of nature, people, and the economy up close and personal, yet in my own comfort zone. That has, I realize now, been a privilege. Plus, I have fallen in love . . . with cows.

AL's SON IS A glorious specimen of the Holstein-Friesian breed valued by today's dairy farmers. His snout is broad with flared nostrils and a beautiful curve. His face is well proportioned and his black-and-white coat is silky, with distinctive patterns. I decide to call him Alfie. I shouldn't, because naming an animal brings it closer to you. And Alfie is destined to leave us.

"Look at the heart shape on its forehead," says Naidu. "It is perfect for people to touch and pray." Rickshaw drivers do this. They pass by a cow, touch its forehead, and press a finger prayerfully to their hearts.

Had he been female, the newborn calf would have made a great addition to the herd. Instead, everyone commiserates with Sarala. "What a waste of effort," they say, clicking their tongues. "Pity it is male."

Two days later, I go with Sarala to see the calf in his cowshed. He lies beside AL, who is chewing her cud meditatively and staring at us. "AL is worried," Sarala says. "She is wondering, 'Why are they here? Are they going to remove my calf?'" Though they are, in fact, going to remove Alfie, one of the other cows has also given birth—to a female, thankfully, which they plan to keep. A third cow is pregnant and will deliver in a few weeks.

"Where is the space, Madam, for me to raise three calves?" asks Sarala, pointing around. The urban cowshed is tight with cows: a far cry from breezy, grassy pastures. At night, Alfie and the newborn female calf may get stomped upon by other cows. But there is no separate enclosure, so Sarala and her family take their chances by leaving the calves with their mothers.

We debate what to do next. We are collective owners of a newborn calf and need to build consensus about his future. Why not sell him, I ask? They look at me with pity. No local dairy farmer will buy a male calf. Of what use is it to him?

What about selling to people who have bullock carts? Maybe this male can be used to pull carts after he grows up?

"This breed is too soft," says Sarala. "HF breeds can't stand the heat and dust of Indian roads, so it can't pull carts."

I shake my head and fantasize about starting a movement against HF cows. Which really has no bearing on the issue at hand—whether or not Sarala and her family can afford to keep Alfie—but dairy farmers in general are too dependent on imported "soft" breeds. Rather than spend money trying to improve the milk yields of the local *Bos indicus* species, the entire system is taking a shortcut by relying wholly on high-yielding but climatically incompatible foreign breeds.

"It all boils down to milk, Madam," says Sarala. "If we had money, if we had savings, you think we wouldn't want to own a native cow or two?

I glare at her. Why does it always boil down to extra milk? "Why don't you take the calf to your village and sell him to people there?"

"Will you give me the transport to take it?" asks Sarala. "Po, ma ["Get out of here" in Tamil]. The cost of our transport will be more than what we will get for the calf."

In villages, she says, where people have grazing pastures, they will simply keep a male calf—much like an unwanted widowed aunt or a crotchety uncle whom you need to take care of. "We can't do that in the city."

Their solution is to take Alfie the calf to a *go-shala* (cow shelter) and leave him there.

"You leave old or ailing cows there, the ones you cannot manage," says Sarala. "They take care of these cows from birth to death."

I am stunned. "But it is a newborn," I say. "How can you abandon a newborn calf? How can you take Alfie away from his mother?"

I have heard about these cow shelters. A tour guide in Mumbai showed me one that operated in the heart of that city, beside the Mahalakshmi Temple. They are usually operated by the Jain community, but I also have seen cow shelters affiliated with cult spiritual groups such as the Hare Krishna temple and the Art of Living Foundation, a global network offering meditation and breathing courses among others. (I took an "AoL course" (as they call it) in New York.)

Sarala and Naidu think that a cow shelter is the best place for an unwanted calf. I am torn about whether to influence their decision and, if so, how. One way I can do it is by throwing money at the problem. It won't take much to subsidize a male calf for a few months, but I doubt that Sarala will use the money I give her to care for Alfie. She will use it to feed the milk-giving cows, and I wouldn't blame her. The economics of dairy farming are skewed in favor of the milking cows. All through this blazing-hot summer, Sarala has been talking about how cruel the heat is on these animals.

"They are hungry," she says often, pointing at her herd. A standing cow is an arresting animal because it can look so still. It can look like the most centered animal on earth. You can do yoga for a million years and you still won't get that unblinking, beguiling gaze. But it still might be starving. "Look at the grass. It is so dry."

Selva wants to keep Alfie for at least a week more. He says that sending the calf away after just a week with its mother doesn't "feel right."

"He likes cows, you see. He wants to hang on to them as long as possible," says Sarala with a proud smile.

Naidu is against this. He says that we should make a clean break between the mother and child. Longer is riskier. The longer we keep the calf with the mother cow, the harder it will be to wean her, to help her forget her baby once we do take the calf away. Naidu is more concerned about the psychology of the mother-cow than the child. The mother is his livelihood. The calf is a freeloader. "After two weeks, she will miss her baby even more," says Naidu. "Once the baby goes, she will develop a fever and perhaps withhold milk throughout the lactating cycle. Best to do it quickly."

Sarala takes the middle road. Some dairy farmers, she says, take the calf away after a single day of colostrum feeding. We have given the calf mother's milk for about a week. That will help build his resistance even if we move him away from his mother, she says.

They are all worried about the butchers. "They will come and steal the calf, Madam," says Naidu. "We have put two locks on the cowshed, but there is no guarantee. They can come at night, break open the lock, and take the calf."

I contemplate keeping Alfie on my balcony. The space is large enough for the tiny calf. Once I get him up the elevator and through the house, it will be easy. Alfie can stand tied to the water pipe. And he can visit his mom every morning and evening during the milkings.

"Your balcony is no better than the go-shala, Madam," says Sarala. "How will the calf stay in your balcony without its mother? You'll have to keep the mother there, too."

A postpregnancy cow is a huge, moody animal. There is no way that I can get AL up my lift and through my living room into the balcony.

Sarala almost clinches it for me by asking one pertinent question: What will you do with the cow dung? Do you know how to remove it?

Why not ask one of the army households to keep Alfie? I suggest the next day. After all, they have land. The calf can be tied up outside a home.

She tried that once, says Sarala. Some years ago, they had a male calf—their first. They didn't want to give it to the cow shelter. Selva wanted to raise it for a few months and then let it loose on the road. "Cows are self-sufficient animals. Once you raise them, they will wander around the neighborhood. They can even forage for food. They may just come to lie down in front of your building." Sarala had asked an army family if they would keep the calf tied outside at night. A few days after the calf was born, she took it one night and tied it to a tree outside one of the army homes.

"Some stray dogs came at night and tore into it. They ate the whole little calf. Only its head was left over when I came the next morning. Can you imagine how I felt? I couldn't sleep for an entire month after that. I got the willies after seeing that poor dead thing. How can a family sleep when a calf is being eaten by dogs, Madam? Didn't they hear the calf bleat?" Sarala shivers.

I have nothing to say.

"You think we give away calves on purpose?" she asks. "We give them away because we have no choice."

Next I suggest sending the calf to the villages where they use bulls for *Jallikattu*, annual events where young men try to hang on to bulls as they run through the village. I have seen this sport in interior Tamil Nadu.

Sarala shakes her head. Jallikattu (which is the Indian version of bull-fighting or rather bull-hugging—bull-clinging, really) is done with native breeds, particularly the Pulikulam breed, she says.

To confirm this, I call Himakiran Anukula, a lover of native breeds, who studied engineering in Wisconsin and returned to India to be an organic farmer. I came across him thanks to a spirited defense of Jallikattu he mounted when the supreme court of India decided to ban the sport, practiced over centuries and millennia in the Madurai region of Tamil Nadu. He confirms that native breeds with humps are the ones used for Jallikattu. Alfie, no matter how willing, would not be welcome. He simply didn't have the "balls" to deal with hundreds of young men high on testosterone.

OVER THE NEXT FEW days Sarala and her family help me get used to the idea of the cow shelter and we finally get on the same page. We will leave the newborn male calf at a go-shala. I agree it is the only option available.

"Don't worry, Madam," says Naidu. "These Jain people take very good care of the cows. It is like being in a cow hotel. You should see them on full moon days. Truckloads of jaggery and other delicacies arrive."

But he knows, and I know, too, that he is merely rationalizing our decision.

On Monday morning, the security guard calls my home. "There is a calf waiting for you," he says. This sounds better in Hindi. I go down and see Alfie standing outside my building gate. He is a gorgeous animal with a pink snout, and wide, alert ears. At that moment, I decide to retract the name I have given him. As if that will help me feel better about having already become attached to this animal that will soon leave my life.

Naidu, his cousin, and a rickshaw-driver friend (who I later discover is half-blind) are with the calf. The rickshaw driver wants fifteen dollars round-trip for dropping off the calf in Whitefield. We settle on ten. We push the calf inside, where he lies on the floor in between Naidu and me. His snout brushes against my calves.

Our first stop is a local office of the cow shelter. There is a process, Sarala has explained to me. First, they have filled out an application form. Then, they show the calf to the local office, where a man will make sure that the calf is indeed theirs, that they haven't stolen him. Only after that can we take Alfie to the cow shelter and leave him, meaning, in my mind, abandon him.

"We need to show the Jain guy this calf and get an authorization form," says Naidu. "Otherwise, they will question whether we stole the calf from somewhere." It doesn't make sense. Why would anyone steal a cow to donate it to a cow shelter? Is Naidu getting some small amount for bringing the calf? I decide not to ask. I am to accompany them to Amar Chand Champalal, a pawnbroker who is also the local officer of the cow shelter. Having me—an educated woman—with them will give them added credibility and ease the calf's way into the shelter. Or that's the plan.

We stop the rickshaw in front of the tiny shop and produce the calf. Amar, a wizened old man clad in a white *kurta* pajama (a long loose tunic on top with pajama-like pants) takes one look at the tiny reluctant animal and waves his assent. He will call the cow shelter and give them a heads-up that we are coming.

"They charge us murderous interest rates for Sarala's wedding chain, the single piece of jewelry we pawn and reclaim," Naidu says ruefully. "And then they go and give the money to places like a cow shelter. Why don't they help us humans?"

"Whatever," says the cousin. "At least they are doing some good work. Let's go."

There are two types of people in the world. Some are animal people and others are not. Both can exist within the same household. To people who aren't into animals, the whole notion of struggling so much with a calf would seem ludicrous. To animal lovers, the fact that we are giving a newborn calf away is outrageous. To both sets of accusers, I say, "You weren't there."

19

THE COW HOTEL

THE SHELTER IS AN hour outside Bangalore proper. Our rickshaw bounces along over flyovers and underpasses. The calf lies at our feet serenely. Soon, we are entering the Bangalore Gorakshan Shala, which translates to "Bangalore Save the Cow Shelter." It is 108 acres of prime land that would be worth millions of dollars if developed. Instead, it is overrun by bovines. In both the Jain and Hindu faiths, 108 is an auspicious number. I doubt that the number of acres bought way back in the 1930s was a coincidence.

There is an arch at the entrance, so it's almost as if we are entering a religious institution. A couple of men sit on the side, napping in their chairs. No one stops or questions us as we walk in pushing a reluctant calf. Cows don't like to be prodded and neither do calves. There is a reason that Taurus, the sign of the bull, is associated with stubbornness. Bovines like to walk at their own pace. Naidu pushes the calf and his cousin pulls it from the front. It takes the two of them to guide the calf into the sprawling space, which is divided into several areas, each with a few hundred cows.

In the front is a large, enclosed area, inside of which seem to be the healthiest animals: a mix of HF cows, native breeds, and bulls. They stand there eating the hay that is spread all over the floor and look up inquiringly as we walk past on our way to the calves' enclave. There are sections for native breeds like the Gir and the Saahil, which come from the North; there is another enclosure, full of black buffaloes with curved horns. In the back are sick cows, with polio or foot-and-mouth disease. There is a gate beyond which, I am told, are the areas where dead cows are buried.

"Look over there! It's a camel. Two camels. Actually four," says the cousin.

On the roofs of the sheds are thousands of doves.

"It costs us thirty thousand dollars a month to run the go-shala," says Kishenlalji Kothari, the secretary of the shelter. Kothari is an elderly man who, like the pawnbroker–local officer we met earlier, is clad in a white *kurta* pajama. White hair sticks out of his ears, which remind me of bovine ears. He reels off a long list of expenses. There are about one thousand cows in the shelter and some four hundred calves. Only about fifty to sixty of them are milking cows. The rest are discards, left by farmers who cannot keep them. Each calf is given a liter of milk a day, bought from milk trucks that stop by daily. Maize and wheat are purchased from local farmers. Even water is expensive. There are about forty-five people on staff, including a doctor, and several other vets on call from the local veterinary college. The shelter runs with contributions from its five hundred members.

"We treat these animals as family members," says Kothari. "It is hard to convince nonvegetarians. They think we are just wasting money. But we don't want to convince them."

Is it because you are a Jain that you do this? I ask Kothari. He demurs. "Being Indians, we consider the cow a sacred animal. We solve their grievances, save them from butchers. In the whole world—not just India—do you know anyone who has not used a product from a cow?"

I think of my vegan friends who eschew all dairy products but nod politely.

The society wants to increase the number of animals to ten thousand, says Kothari. They dream of using fifty of their acres for the cow shelter and then building hospitals, orphanages, and old-age homes—for humans, not necessarily cows—in the remaining land. The goal is that their cow shelter becomes not just self-sufficient but also able to support other shelters all over India. They want to educate farmers to value animals.

"Everything I am is because of the blessing of the cow," says Kothari. "If you think about it, the cow is the most evolved animal, after humans."

"What about chimpanzees?" I ask.

"Chimpanzees don't give milk to humans. They aren't generous like cows."

I'd like to refute him but don't know enough about chimps to do so. I make a mental note to read Jane Goodall.

Kothari challenges me to think of a goal that I want to attain.

"I'd like to be a stand-up comic," I say.

He frowns. He was hoping for a more serious goal, I can tell. "Pray to the holy cow and if you attain your goal, if you get some peace of mind, support us a little," he says.

Naidu and I are not peaceful at the calves' enclosure. We are distressed. Naidu looks around, wondering where to leave our calf. He leads it to a vacant spot and quickly ties its rope to the pillar. A neighboring calf comes forward and smells the new entrant inquiringly. Cows, they say, have a keen sense of smell. They can smell things miles away. But not their own dung, perhaps. How else can they stand amid their excrement?

The tied calf stands there uncertainly. The other animals look fairly healthy. There is the odd calf that is lying on the ground, gasping for breath, clearly sick. Blood is seeping out of another calf's rear. But for the most part, the calves are standing, sitting, napping, and bleating. They don't look deprived or abused.

A huge truck comes in. Two men begin to unload hay. The calf is still standing. It doesn't bleat reproachfully at us. What do we do? Are we doing the right thing? Naidu and I watch our calf anxiously for a few minutes. And then, decisively, we turn and walk away.

We do not look back.

THE NEXT MORNING, BOTH Sarala and I are strained as we meet for milk. "We have left the calf," I say, nay accuse. "Just as you wanted."

"I know. That rickshaw driver fleeced you. He is half-blind and is collecting money for his eye operation," says Sarala. "Did you tell the staff to take special care of our calf?"

"I just followed your husband's lead. He didn't speak to anyone about caring for AL's calf and neither did I. I did talk with the secretary of the whole society," I tell her. Perhaps I can get him to instruct his staff to take special care.

Sarala shakes her head. "Doesn't work like that, Madam," she tells me. "He may do it. But do you think the woman or man taking care of that particular cow pen is going to care, caught up as they are in the daily and hourly urgencies of tending to these animals? I wouldn't."

A bottom-up approach, in other words, would have been better.

"That wastrel husband of mine knows nothing," Sarala continues. "Why didn't you say something, Madam? You should have slipped fifty or one hundred rupees to the staff and told them to take care of our little one. They do that if you ask for it. They will even brand your calf with an iron so that you can identify it when it grows up. That is painful for our baby so we don't need to do any branding. But, at least, you should have told them to look after it."

"I thought your husband would do all that," I reply. "How would I know?"

We bicker with each other—feeling bad, laying blame.

"I didn't sleep at all last night," says Sarala. "I was thinking about the calf the whole time. Look at its mother."

AL is mooing loudly and apparently has been for the last hour. She looks hither and thither, searching for her calf. Had he been around, he would have mooed in reply. AL doesn't stop.

A milkman I have never seen approaches AL with his pail. Selva has left town, says Sarala. He hates it when they give away animals. He runs away. They have hired a milkman to do the job today. All of them are exhausted and sad. But the cows need to be milked.

Sarala walks along with the milkman and stands in front of AL, "making nice," as she calls it. She rubs AL's forehead and ears, speaking softly. Two of AL's teats are not working. They need to call the vet. Sarala plans to take AL to the grassy meadow inside the army compound. They are worried that AL will develop a fever. This is what happens to cows when they are sad.

Studies about animal emotions are frequently conflicting. Everyone has a view. Some studies have found, for instance, that cows with names give more milk. The idea is that naming a cow changes the farmer's behavior towards it, makes it more personalized, and reduces the stress on the cow, which in turn leads to increased milk production. So it's not just people who get more attached with a name, as I feared with Alfie. The cows are affected, too. In 2011, a researcher at Northampton University in the UK found that cows have complex social and emotional lives. Their heart rates went up when they were separated from the herd, and they formed bonds with certain animals. Cows even have best friends, the Northhampton study indicated.

Sarala agrees. "Cows are like humans, she tells me. They form relationships. They feel pain. They can't speak. That's the only difference." Sarala continues in this vein, verbalizing my thoughts, wondering out loud if the calf slept last night and how it is faring without its mother. "If the calf goes to suckle other cows, they will kick its face with their hind legs," she says. "Poor thing, it has to receive this abuse at first before it can latch on to another cow-mother."

Not all scientists climb onto the "animals have emotions" bandwagon. The usual criticism is that humans anthropomorphize animals, attributing human qualities to them. As I study the research on cows and emotions, I learn that calves separated from their mothers quickly forge new connections with other cows. The mother will miss the calf for some time but will adjust far quicker than a human mother who has been separated from her baby. I know this with dogs. When a litter is given away, the mother dog perhaps mourns for a while but life returns to normal soon enough. This knowledge gives me hope that AL will cope fine without her calf.

Still, I take home my milk feeling terrible. No matter how much I tell myself otherwise, I cannot help thinking that I have failed—betrayed—the newborn calf and its mother. Have I committed a sin? Should I not have gotten involved?

The next day, too, AL moos loudly for her calf. I wake up to her mooing and observe her from my balcony. I fill up the bucket with fruit and vegetable peels and take it downstairs. Usually I divide the contents of the bucket between several cows, who all look at me as I cross the street. This time, I head straight for AL and dump the entire contents of the bucket at her feet. She stops mooing and eats.

After breakfast, I decide to go back to the cow shelter. I am not sure what I am after, but I want to check on the calf. I phone Sarala to ask if she wants to come with me. Milking over, she accepts eagerly.

It is noon when we reach the shelter. All the calves are re-arranged. I wonder if I can find our calf. We poke around and find him a few yards from his original location. He is sitting down desultorily. He doesn't jump and bound towards us when he sees us. Cows aren't demonstrative like that, says Sarala. Instead, our calf stays in his place, staring unblinkingly at us. He looks okay. Thank God!

We bend down and give the calf the goodies that we have brought: jaggery, bananas, coconut shreds, grass, hay. A thin, dark woman in a cotton sari walks up. She is part of the staff at the shelter. I offer her a box of sweets that I have brought—a clumsy attempt at a bribe.

"Please take care of this one," I say, pointing at my calf.

The woman stares at me. "They come one day and go the next," she says. "Some people bring the calf just a day after birth. How will it survive? It will catch an infection."

"Ours is seven days old," Sarala tells her. "Please put a red thread or a rope around its neck so we can identify it as it grows."

The woman takes the sweet box wordlessly and walks away.

Satisfied that the calf is okay, we walk to the main enclosure. A massive vaccination exercise is going on. A veterinarian holds an injection in his hand while four men—actually two boys and two men corral the cows, one after another. "It is to protect them against foot-and-mouth disease," says the vet. "Once they contract that, we cannot do anything." They grab each animal with a rope and bring it to the wicket fence where the doctor waits. He inserts the needle into the rump of each struggling cow. Animals in fear all exhibit similar responses. I've seen it in my dog and I see it here with the cows. Each cow arches away from the hypodermic-wielding vet, its mouth frothing with saliva and the whites of its eyes visible. The intensity of its response—the wild, fearful, frothing reaction and crazed eyes—is out of proportion to the simple pinprick of the injection. Then again, the animal doesn't know that beforehand. As far as it is concerned, capture leads to bad things, ranging from a ride in a tightly packed van to a butcher's block to an injection. Uncertainty is what the animal is reacting to, not the injection.

We are loath to leave, and yet we need to go. In an hour, my kids will be home from school and Sarala has put aside innumerable responsibilities. We go back to see the calf again. I kneel down in front of him.

Crows fly above in circles, dispensing malaise and hope in equal parts. A camel watches us from a distance, its head fluffed and coiffed like a cool socialite.

"I am sorry," I whisper, kneeling beside the calf. Even though I have renounced his name, I can't help calling him Alfie. I stroke his back. I hate goodbyes. Always have. Goodbyes are guilt on steroids.

"You are going to be okay." The words sound hollow, even to my ears.

He looks up. His eyes aren't accusing, merely inquiring. Calves are like cows, except a hundred times more innocent.

"You are going to be okay," I repeat.

So saying, I get up and walk away from Alfie, who I am abandoning—no getting away from that—at a cow shelter outside Bangalore.

20

FINDING A BRIDE

I'D LIKE TO TELL you that we thought about the calf every day. We didn't. Sarala and I talked about Alfie for a while—often in the beginning and then occasionally. Life goes on. The silk-cotton tree's leaves fall. Its pods split open. Squirrels and parrots eat the cottony puffs inside. Saucer-like seeds float to the ground. A few months pass.

One day I walk by the statue of Mother Mary at the entrance to the narrow gully where Sarala lives. On a whim, I go into the tiny lane and ask people for Sarala's house. I have never been here. They tell me that she has moved to near the Tamil Sangam. The next day, when I get my milk, I ask her why. She says that they needed to move to a better home so that they could find a bride.

Sarala is looking for brides for her middle two sons. One is in the Indian army and the other works for an IT company. They are well educated, she says. She wants an educated daughter-in-law, "with at least a master's degree" for her thirty- and thirty-four-year-old boys. Part of the reason they are having trouble finding brides for their middle two sons is because parents don't want their daughters to be married into a dairy-farming household.

Every now and then, she goes for a few days to her native village, Arni, to scout out girls who will be comfortable with the rhythms of her family and the cows. Not that they will need to be intimately involved with cow rearing or dairy, Sarala clarifies. The elder of the two sons is posted in Kashmir.

"Will the girl go up North? Near Pakistan?" I ask.

"Why not, Madam? We will just send a cow or two with her. It will make her feel at home. Plus the North Indian hay and grass is probably fresher and stronger than the grass here. The cows will come back as beauties."

"Sarala, you are only thinking about the cows," I caution. "You just said that the brides these days don't want to be mixed up with cows."

"Yes, yes," Sarala says, scowling. She still resents this new reality even as she is resigned to it. "Selva should not have all these problems when we look for a bride for him."

The family is trying to get Selva out of milking. They want him to take a proper job with an office and a salary. It will be a double whammy for Selva if the girl's family finds out that not only is his family in milking, but that it's his job, too.

"The parents think that we will put their daughters to work—cleaning up cow dung and washing the cows, you see. They don't want their daughters to be doing such menial work. Now everyone wants to work in an office, even girls in my village," says Sarala with a touch of pique.

Milking is not an easy profession. Sarala accepts that. The physical labor is daunting: both tedious and smelly. You wake up to feed the cows at 4:30 a.m., milk them, refill their water buckets at 1 p.m., clean up their dung, milk them in the evening, and put them to bed in their cowshed.

"We want Selva to have a better life. All through his childhood, we tried to talk him out of this milking life," she says. "We actually got a policeman to beat him up to make him take a different job when he was a teenager. Even construction. But the lad flatly refused. He loves those cows and wants to make a livelihood from them." She smiles approvingly, almost in spite of herself.

Sarala is in a quandary. She is consumed by the bride-search for her sons. They have relocated to live away from the cowshed, so that potential brides and their families won't see the cows, which are still tied in front of their old home. Yet at the same time Sarala resents the bad rap that dairy farming is getting in the matrimonial circuit.

"It is good karma, after all, to work with cows," I say.

"Karma is all very well but it doesn't fill your stomach," says Sarala, knowing that after years of this futile bride-search, she must come to terms with the new reality. When all her customers have left, Sarala and I take a walk. "There must be some connection between cows and our family. Else why would we be in this profession generation after generation—my father, grandfather, my husband, and now my son? We must have taken something from those animals in past lives and so we must spend this life doing service to them."

There is one glimmer of hope. The following week, Sarala plans to go to her village and meet a family with two sisters. She is optimistic about "finishing off the matchmaking" and is hoping to set it up so that the two sisters can marry two brothers—her sons. It will reduce family quarrels.

Suddenly she asks, "Do you want to come with me?"

I don't know what to say.

"If you come, we can go in your car. I can reach Arni and return in one day. I don't need to find someone to take care of the cows. Otherwise, I have to pay someone. It will also give you a nice chance to see the country. Breathe some fresh air."

I nod, trying to figure out if I have the time for a road trip.

"You have two daughters," says Sarala. "If you help me get my sons married, the gods will shower their blessings on you. Your girls will find good husbands."

What mother can resist setting off a chain reaction, however nebulous, that will end up in a good spouse for her child? My friend Jana says that in the Jewish faith, if you arrange a match, you are assured a place in heaven.

"Distance from Bangalore to Arni," I type into my computer. It takes four hours. Sarala says that if we leave at seven—"after sending your kids to school," she adds considerately—we can reach Arni by eleven, meet the prospective brides' family, have lunch somewhere else, and return.

"Why not have lunch at the girls' house?" I ask. "We can eat and talk. Get to know them a bit."

"Oh no," says Sarala, shaking her head vehemently. "We never eat at the brides' house till the marriage happens. They will think we are freeloaders. Don't worry. There are other good places we can eat. Clean, vegetarian."

We leave right after the kids get on the school bus. Ram is out of town. I warn Sarala many times that we will have to be back by nightfall. My Toyota Innova is full. Naidu and my driver Robert sit in front. Sarala and I are in the middle. The back is full of gifts for her family: sacks of rice; woven baskets full of vegetables, fruits, and flowers; and a clucking chicken in a cage. Apparently, it was born in Arni. Sarala wants to take it back to reconnect it to its mother. They may kill it after the reunion, she says. "Let it die happy, after seeing its mother for the last time."

There are a ton of birds en route: white egrets, pied kingfishers, coppersmith barbets, and parakeets, all uniformly hated by farmers, says Sarala, because they stir up and swallow seeds. Every field has a scarecrow made out of sticks and old sacks. There are beehives, mating dragonflies, and molting butterflies. Village boys jump naked into flowing rivers. Turbaned farmers plough the fields by walking behind two bullocks. We drive through country lanes bordered by ancient trees that arch over the road.

Sarala's village is ridiculously verdant, surrounded by paddy fields, banana trees, and vegetable patches so green they could put an emerald to shame. A single street with mud houses painted in riotous colors of peacock blue, lime green, and brick red. A backyard garden with homegrown vegetables. Cows tied in the cowshed out back. Roosters crowing, hens clucking, chickens running around like crazy. It is a happy place. Why did they ever move to the city?

Sarala echoes my thoughts. "I don't know why we ever moved to the city."

Some ten families live in the village. All are related to Sarala through generations. The main activities and sources of income are farming and cattle rearing. The men farm; the women take care of the animals. During the summers, they pat down dough made of *urad* (a type of lentil) and specked with broken black pepper and cumin. These *papads* are dried in the sun, bound, and sold at cooperatives. Families in the city buy them and fry them in oil like fritters.

A platoon of people waits to receive us. We must be the entertainment, I think at first. But really, it is a measure of the affection that they have for Sarala. And the gifts that she brings, too, I suppose.

The first thing we pull out of the car is the chicken, clucking loudly in its bamboo cage. Sarala takes the cage into the backyard and lets the chicken loose. It races towards the group of birds in a raucous homecoming. We carry baskets of vegetables and fruits into the cool, bare interior. Village homes are minimal and clutter-free. There is bedding rolled up in one end of the dark living room and braided mats rolled out for us to sit cross-legged on the floor. Someone brings out a mud pot of water and pours us each a glass. A man cuts some tender coconut and shaves off its top before handing us the coconut water.

Sarala and her relatives talk nonstop about the trip and the visit. "Have you told the girls' people that we are coming?" asks Sarala.

"Don't worry. It is all arranged," says her brother. "We are going to see them before lunch. During the auspicious time. Today it is from twelve to one thirty."

A boy is dispatched on a bike to tell the brides' side that we have arrived.

At first, Sarala's relatives view me with mild suspicion: the city lady. None of them speaks English, but my fluent Tamil puts them at ease. Though they speak Telugu at home, they live in Tamil Nadu, so they know Tamil. Soon we are joking like old friends.

We drink coffee. Do I want to go out to the backyard to pick vegetables? Sarala's elder brother, a gaunt man with coffee-black skin, asks if I'd like to see the whole village.

Sarala intervenes on my behalf. "Let her drink coffee first," she says. "Why are you folks hurrying her like this?"

"First drink your coffee, Madam," she tells me. "Then I will show you the cowshed."

The children stare unblinkingly at me as I down my coffee, village-style, with the outwardly curved rim of the stainless steel tumbler not touching my lips, yet perfect for pouring the liquid down my throat. No sipping. That is uncouth and impolite.

Later we walk through the cowshed—Sarala, her brother, and I—where some fifteen cows are tethered. Sarala has names for and stories about each one. These animals have been part of her family for generations, she says; their ancestors are linked to hers, with each bovine generation feeding a human one.

"Do you see the difference between these cows and the city ones?" asks Sarala.

Sure, I say, pointing at their humps. These are native breeds, not the foreign Holstein-Friesian or Jersey breeds.

"They are like our brothers and sisters," says Sarala, scratching a reddish-brown cow. The cow stares back. I follow suit, stroking her neck and scratching the tender skin behind her ears.

"You remember Kamala, don't you?" says Sarala's brother. "See how much she has grown?"

The cow stamps. "Kamala was so attached to my father, poor thing," Sarala tells me. "And it went both ways. My dad wouldn't eat till he fed Kamala jaggery. Every single day. When my father was on his deathbed, Kamala tore off the rope that we used to tether her here and ran to our house. She sensed that her master was dying, you see. She stood outside my father's bedroom window, without moving, for hours till my father passed away in the wee hours of night. She knew that he had died even before any of us knew. She mooed with such agony that it roused the whole household. I was dozing beside my father's bed. When I heard her moo, I knew, even without looking, that my dad was gone."

The cowshed is a simple construction, with a thatched roof and mud floor. Bamboo poles hold aloft the roof, except in the back where a brick wall has been built to shelter the cows, or so I think. When we walk outside, I see the real reason for the brick wall: all along the other side are cow-dung patties, stuck like buttons on the wall, drying in the sun.

Wet cow dung is a mess—about the consistency of, well, shit. Here, it is mixed with dry hay to give it the consistency of pizza dough, rolled, and then thrown onto the brick wall so that it dries in the sun—after which it will be used as kindling for fires. Rolling a ball of cow dung and throwing it on a wall involves dexterity, good judgment about the girth of the ball, and a measure of aim. Sarala is good at this but her brother is better. He squats on the ground, swiftly picks up a handful of cow dung and hay, lobs it up and down to shape it into a circle, and then throws it at the wall without even looking. No gloves, no rake, nothing. It makes me squirm to watch him and lends credence to the belief that the human mind can get used to just about anything. Even stinking cow-dung balls.

I watch as the dung sticks to the wall. It is all about balancing gravity and surface tension. If the cow-dung ball is too heavy, gravity pulls it down and it falls off. If the amount of dung is too little, surface tension will not hold it attached to the wall. It has to be just the right amount. Sarala's brother is also, no surprise, a great ballplayer.

By now, the sun is high in the sky. After walking around some more, it is time for lunch. We sit cross-legged on the floor. A banana leaf is spread out. We eat plantain chips, fried in coconut oil; steaming-hot, red-specked rice, aged in gunnysacks for years; okra sambhar; a dollop of ghee; and several cooked vegetables, freshly picked from the garden. It is the tastiest food I have ever eaten—redolent of Eleven Madison Park, Daniel, The French Laundry, or Jean Georges. Well, those are bad comparisons, for this is rustic food, but any chef concerned with terroir would have loved it.

The flavor comes from slow-cooking the local, freshly picked produce in mud pots over a wood fire. Also, when you serve hot rice and ghee on a banana leaf, it imparts a herbaceous complement, somewhat like what New Zealanders claim about their sauvignon blancs. The women clean up—a sexist exercise steeped in tradition, not just in India but most rural areas. When I rise to help, they all demur but don't complain too much.

We pick up the banana-leaf "plates" and dump them into an open compost pit. Sarala's pretty cousin, Sita, picks up a blob of cow dung and tosses it into a bucket. To this, she adds half a bucket of water. Deftly, Sita dribbles the cow dung water all over the floor. She takes a piece of cloth, begins at the top, bends, and sweeps the floor with her hand, creating neat curves on the floor, all with the cow dung paste. I am once again reminded of my cousin Kicha and his Mr. Muscle bottle. Nobody walks on the floor till the paste dries into a solid, greenish-hued substrate atop the already-greenish-hued floor. This is where we will have dinner later that evening, sitting atop the cow-dung-laced mud floor for another meal on a banana leaf.

I can hear the women laughing in the back. Huge peals of it come from the kitchen, loud and free. They have a grace about them, these village women, a sense of leisure and wellness. I attribute it to the homegrown, organic food.

But, as one study shows, perhaps it is the cow dung. *Mycobacterium vaccae* is a bacteria first discovered in cow dung in Austria. The word *vaccae* is Latin for "cow dung." Research has shown that exposure to these bacteria can make people smarter and less depressed. I am not kidding. Two biology professors from Russell Sage College in Troy, New York, presented this finding at a 2010 meeting of the American Society for Microbiology. It was reported with the telling headline, "Can Bacteria Make You Smarter?" *Mycobacterium vaccae* occurs naturally in soil and cow dung. People who spend time amidst nature and cows are likely to ingest or breathe it in, writes Dorothy Matthews, who conducted this research with her colleague Susan Jenks.

When these bacteria were ingested by mice, it stimulated the growth of neurons that cause increasing levels of serotonin—the feel-good hormone—and thus decreased anxiety in the mice. Since serotonin plays a role in learning, Matthews wondered if *M. vaccae* could improve learning in mice. Turns out it could. The mice that ingested the bacteria navigated a maze twice as fast and with less anxiety than the control group. Sarala's relatives wipe their floors daily with cow dung and ingest the bacteria while they eat. No wonder they laugh so hard. It is the serotonin induced by the cow-dung bacteria, layered over the floor after every meal over years and years.

⁂

SARALA AND HER FAMILY have gone and seen the two sisters. They come back subdued.

"Their faces are shaped weirdly, Madam," says Naidu. "We cannot get our boys married to girls with odd-shaped faces."

Sarala too is oddly silent. She takes me aside and says, "Do you mind if we leave right away?"

I nod my head.

"Naidu is right," she says and then immediately contradicts herself. "But he is impractical."

By now, I am used to this. Sarala's world is never black and white, right and wrong. It is all about gradations and tradeoffs, choosing between imperfect solutions.

"These village girls won't work for my boys. They are country breeds, you see. My boys are crossbreeds. It will be hard if I marry a native cow to them. Won't set. But the thing is that these girls are sisters. They will have each other for company—to complain about their husbands. It may work. Plus, how long to keep on searching for a bride for these boys? We still have Selva to get married off."

I cannot tell if she intends to pursue the alliance or not. After saying goodbye, we load the van with baskets of peanuts, chickens, and fresh produce. Sarala promises to return in a few weeks.

21

THREE WEDDINGS AND A PASSING

SOME MONTHS LATER, SARALA shows up at my door with a wedding invitation. She has decided on the two sisters for her middle two boys, she says cheerily. The wedding is in their village. I look at the date and apologize right away. I have a work trip that I cannot cancel, I tell Sarala. She doesn't seem too upset, maybe because I don't know her middle two boys. So I put a cash gift for each of the boys in an envelope, beg my kids to create a happy wedding-day card—on which they draw elaborate flowers, birds, and the sun rising between the hills—and take it to Sarala across the street. She genially protests and then accepts the envelope.

Sarala and I don't see each other for a while after that. She doesn't come to the milking spot regularly. Naidu tells me that

Sarala is busy with wedding preparations. Only Selva comes. He is the object of much good-natured teasing.

"After your two elder brothers get married, it's your turn," say the army wives. "Just you wait. Your parents will finish off your marriage before you blink."

Selva has mellowed. He merely grins when we gang up on him. No snarls or scowls from him these days.

TWO YEARS PASS IN a flurry of transitions. My elder daughter graduates from high school and leaves for college in the United States. When my father-in-law becomes sick, my in-laws give up their home in Kerala and move into a furnished apartment in our building complex. We drop off my daughter at Carnegie Mellon in Pittsburgh, where she wants to study engineering. I stop buying milk from Sarala. There is less time to walk across the street. It is easier to buy packet milk.

I notice only two cows come these days. I see them when I walk my younger daughter to school in the morning. I never see Sarala, and Selva, too, has stopped coming. In his place is an old man who wears a checked blue *lungi* (sarong) to squat and milk. Naidu stands next to him, talking desultorily. The customers who once thronged around Sarala have been reduced to a trickle.

I usually wave at Naidu from across the street, but one day I go over to catch up. Selva is driving an auto-rickshaw these days, says Naidu. They want a "respectable" profession for him. They are readying him for a good marriage. I had assumed Sarala was either visiting her village to scout for a bride or staying home to take care of her grandson, but Naidu informs me that they have rented a Seven Eleven–type corner shop and that Sarala is manning it.

"We only have four cows now," he says. "I take care of them all."

"Is my cow there?" I ask, worried that they may have sold her or, worse, that she has died.

Naidu smiles. "Of course, Madam. She is the best milker. Why don't you go the cowshed and have a look at her?"

"I won't recognize her," I say.

"She will recognize you."

I nod. It is too complicated to explain to him that I have no time to go to the cowshed. And we are all petrified of catching infections these days, lest we pass it on to my father-in-law.

"Tell Sarala I asked after her," I say.

"You should go and see the shop," replies Naidu.

Sarala's shop is right behind my apartment complex, he says, on the main road across from Ulsoor Lake.

ONE DECEMBER MORNING, MY father-in-law passes away. The rituals we perform after his death link me once again back to cows. Different cultures and religions deal with grief differently. We all discover that Hinduism is very forward-looking, quite literally. After cremating the dead, for instance, the living are instructed to walk away without looking back. Another ritual involves sprinkling ashes in holy rivers. We choose the nearby Kaveri River and drive two hours with my father-in-law's ashes in tow. There, too, the priest tells Ram to go shoulder-deep into the water, throw the clay pot containing the ashes over his head, and return to shore without looking back.

Every day, the priest comes to our home for an hour of morning services. On the fifth day, he recites Sanskrit mantras and rolls a coconut on the floor. The coconut is in lieu of a cow, he says. "You can catch the tail of a cow and walk all the way up to the heavens," he says. "That is why a cow is so important in Hinduism."

Hindu mythology (the *Garuda Purana*, to be precise) describes a river called Vaitharani that lies between the earth and the world of Yama, the Hindu god of death. It is similar to the river Styx in Greek mythology or the Sanzu River in Japanese Buddhist mythology—a watery passage that souls must cross on their way to heaven. The Vaitharani, though, is fear-inducing: full of blood, pus, crocodiles, moss, stench, whirlpools, and bones, and surrounded by flesh-eating birds. Sinners have a tough time even contemplating navigating it.

There are a few things, though, that can help all of us: fasting on certain holy days, like Ekadasi and Sivarathri, and doing good deeds, such as donating a cow. If we wish, says the priest, he can arrange for a cow donation. There is a village outside Bangalore that is full of Brahmin dairy farmers. He can arrange to take us there to donate a cow.

My husband says that we will consider it and we leave it at that. He does not say, "Been there, done that!"

SOME MONTHS LATER, I go for an evening walk to the nearby Ulsoor Lake when a familiar voice hails me.

"Madam, how are you?" exclaims Sarala from inside a small shop.

I stop in my tracks and grin at her. We are delighted to see each other. Sarala ushers me into the tiny space and plies me with food and drink: a bottle of soda, some chocolates, orange juice, tea, all in succession. I say no, but she hands me the bottle of juice and insists that I take it home. She asks after my family. Somehow she knows that my father-in-law has passed away. One of the building security guards mentioned it to Naidu, who told her, she says. She offers her condolences and we sit quietly together.

Finally I ask after her family. Sarala is bursting with news.

"Do you know? I have readied a bride for Selva," says Sarala proudly. "She is my elder brother's daughter."

"How so?" I ask, knowing that "elder brother" can mean "distant cousin" in the convoluted context of Indian relationships.

It turns out to be exactly that. Sarala's distant cousin has a daughter who is now betrothed to Selva.

"Did Selva and the girl know each other? Were they childhood playmates?" I ask.

"No, he didn't know her. She is a village girl, you see."

Sarala shows me a photo of the girl. She is wearing a blue sari and is slim and lovely looking. I tell Sarala and Naidu, who has just come in, so.

They nod and sigh, and I get the feeling that they aren't quite thrilled with the match but are making the best of the situation. Selva, whom I have known for ten years, is now twenty-eight. Time for him to get married.

What needs to be done? I ask. How can I help?

The financials around Selva's wedding dictate its location. If they pay four thousand rupees (sixty dollars), the priest at a local temple will officiate and conduct all the religious rituals. After that, they plan to host a lunch for some one hundred fifty people at the Tamil Sangam building, which stands right beside their shop.

As we speak, a crowd of customers keeps coming and going. Like at the milking station, Sarala has complex relationships with her customers. One couple spends half an hour with her, negotiating the price of a spare counter-table that she has at home. They want to start a shop just like Sarala's but don't have the money. The wife says that she plans to take her gold wedding chain to the pawnshop and get cash. Sarala and Naidu give them advice and tips. Make sure that the gold chain has proper markings, says Sarala. Else, these pawnbrokers will palm off an inferior copy of your chain when you go back to retrieve it. Naidu promises to hook up the young man with Senthil, who has experience renting shops.

A young college girl who looks like my daughter comes in to buy Pepsi. Sarala pulls out a Coke bottle from the fridge. She picks the bottles by color, not lettering. "The other brown bottle, Auntie," says the girl. As Sarala fumbles inside the fridge, the girl adds, "Okay, why don't you give me a green Sprite bottle?"

"Why don't you eat properly instead of drinking all this sugary junk?" says Sarala.

Two army wives come to get milk from the familiar stainless-steel bucket that Sarala has placed behind the counter. "Even if I move away, these army ladies will not leave me," she says with a grin.

The army wives and I catch up as well. It is just like being back at the milking station with Sarala. They are aghast that I have sent my (unmarried) daughter away to America. "Why would you send your girl all alone to a place so far away?" asks one.

"You cannot trust that country," says another. My shoulders stiffen as I feel another round of what my brother calls "too-brutal honesty" coming on. "Just you watch. Your daughter will show up with a boyfriend. It is all too common in that land."

Sarala comes to my rescue. "It is getting common even here," she says. "My kids and your kids may agree to arranged marriages, but all these school kids who come to my shop—for them, boyfriend-girlfriend is the norm."

She admonishes a student in school uniform when he asks for a cigarette. "Why don't you spend your money on textbooks instead?" she says.

Cigarettes are the most popular item. Young men and women buy a single cigarette, sometimes two or four, sometimes menthol, but never a full pack, which, at two hundred fifty rupees—about four dollars—is expensive for the student types that I see in the store. Sarala says that she does a good business in cigarettes, to the point where the cigarette companies have given her the fridge and flat-screen TV inside the shop. A candy company paid for the gaudy awning in front with dark and gold chocolate and the words *Cadbury's Milk Chocolate* written across it.

"You will come for Selva's wedding, won't you?" Sarala asks. It is a month away.

I wouldn't miss it for the world. As I get ready to leave, I remember something that Ram has been wanting to do.

"I am looking for a go-shala with native cows," I tell Sarala. "I don't want to go far away. Do you know any?"

I don't tell her that my husband and I want to do something for native Indian cows—not the HF ones that Sarala owns—in my father-in-law's memory.

"Go to the Hare Krishna ashram," says Sarala immediately. "Near Hebbal. It is full of desi cows."

THE HARE KRISHNA ASHRAM has a small go-shala—only a dozen cows, but each is a beauty. There are four Gir cows from Gujarat with shiny, red skin, drooping ears, and sweet dispositions. Ram and I tell the monk sitting behind a counter right next to the cows that we want to do something in my father-in-law's name. There are many options. We can feed one cow for a day or year, or five cows or the entire herd for a specific number of days. We choose to feed the entire herd for three days. I spend fifteen minutes nuzzling the Gir cows. I have not seen such gorgeous specimens even at all the places I visited with Sarala.

The monk offers us some of their milk. "It is like *amrit*," he says. The nectar of immortality.

I buy two liters, go home, and boil it. The next day, I try it with my morning coffee. The monk is right. Not too thick or too thin, just fragrant enough, the milk is balanced just right.

It is delicious.

POSTSCRIPT

SELVA'S WEDDING DAY DAWNS in the usual way: temple bells clanging, cows mooing, cars honking, and crows cawing. "Good you came," says Sarala, beaming at me. "It is only a few of us here. The rest will come for lunch."

Selva is wearing a white silk shirt and matching dhoti. A garland made of white tuberoses and sequins lies loosely around his shoulders. Beside him is the bride, wearing a bright-red silk sari with gold borders. She, too, has a garland and lots of jewelry: bangles, necklaces, waistband, armband, rings, the kind I wore for my wedding.

The priest ushers the couple into the sanctum sanctorum of the temple, right in front of the gods.

After we eat I find Selva by himself, standing in a corner, speaking on the phone.

I wait to say goodbye to him.

"That was my elder brother," he says in explanation. "He couldn't come from up north to attend the wedding."

"It was a good wedding. You have a nice wife," I reply.

He smiles shyly.

I change the topic.

"What gift shall we give you?" I ask Selva. "Shall all of us—the army wives and my family—pool together and buy you a cow?"

Now he grins. "They are trying to get me out of the milking business and you all want to buy me a cow?" he says. "I am driving a rickshaw these days."

I smile back at him. "The times, they are a-changing," I say.

After a pause, Selva confides. "What I really want to do is get a cab on lease and drive for those car companies. You know, like Uber."

"Oh, really?" I ask, surprised that he would mention the most valued stock in the world.

Later that night, over dinner, I ask Ram a question. "How much will it cost to fund a small cab? A Hyundai or Nissan?"

My husband looks up from his plate and gives me a look—*the* look.

"What?" I ask defensively, as married folk are wont to do.

"Nothing," he replies in dulcet tones. "We just need to look into Uber's terms and conditions."

ACKNOWLEDGMENTS

ONE OF THE PLEASURES of writing a book is that you get to acknowledge the various strands of people and ideas that went into it.

My first acknowledgment goes to the milkmen and milkwomen whom I consulted throughout the writing of this book and who form its anchor and spine. Even though they don't read this language, they were generous with their thoughts and ideas. My greatest thanks must go to them, and most particularly to Sarala, Naidu, Selva, Senthil, and Sarala's extended family.

This book began with a series of articles for *Mint Lounge*. I thank R. Sukumar, and Priya Ramani for the editorial carte blanche that they gave me while writing that series. Raju Narisetti, the founding editor of *Mint*, has always been a cheerleader of my ideas.

Small sections of the book came from a piece I wrote about Bangalore for *Condé Nast Traveler*. I thank Ted Moncreiff, my editor, for his support.

For history and mythology about the cow, I thank Shatavadhani R. Ganesh, Vrinda Acharya, T. S. Sathyavathi, K. S. Kannan, Shankar Rajaraman, Michel Danino, Bibek Debroy, Naresh Keerthi, Venetia Ansell, Skanda, Shashi Kiran, Ramaswamy Sastry of Vedadhara Trust, and other Sanskrit scholars who have guided and corrected my knowledge on cows through their books, writings, and conversations. Those who would like to read about how the cow plays a role in Hindu ritual and thought need only to read the un-abridged versions of the *Mahabharata* by Ganguli or Debroy, and the voluminous Brahmana literature, particularly the *Shatapatha Brahmana*.

For information about desi cows, I thank Sajal Kulkarni, Sopan Joshi, Monica Sodhi of the NDDB, Himakiran Anugula, Aparna Pallavi, Pon Dheepankar, Sagari R. Ramdas, Dr. Shantha Raman of Jain's Cow Urine clinic, and Jahnavi Pai.

I read and used the research of the following people: Aparna Pallavi's articles in *Down to Earth* (downtoearth.org); Sopan Joshi's article "Why Is the Cow a Political Animal?" for *Yahoo News*; Jay Mazoomdaar's piece "The Desi Cow: Almost Extinct," for *Tehelka* magazine; D. N. Jha's *The Myth of the Holy Cow*; Jan Houben's *Violence Denied: Violence, Non-violence, and the Rationalization of Violence Amongst South Asians*; and Ashutosh Varshney's "Return of the Cow" column, among others.

For books, I recommend *The Study of Cow in Sanskrit Literature* by a scholar with the magnificently long name Bogavarrapu Venkata Vishweshwara Sita Rama Sharma or B. V. V. S. R. Sharma; *Kangayam Breed of Cattle* by Dr. B. Pattabhiraman (available at Krishikosh.egranth.ac.in); "Profile of Livestock Keepers (Breed Savior Awardees 2010)," by Seva, an NGO (available at Sevango.in).

My brother and sister-in-law, Shyam and Priya Sunder, and their children, Sangeeta and Harsha, opened up their home to us for over a year when we first moved to Bangalore. They taught us the ropes about life in India and in Bangalore with tremendous grace, generosity, and affection. It is hard to imagine our life without their constant, entertaining, and reassuring presence.

My brother-in-law, Krishnan, an internist by training has been studying epigraphy and ancient Indian texts for years. His knowledge of and help with translations of the *Shatapata Brahmana* and *Apasthamba Dharmasutra* was invaluable. My sister-in-law, Lakshmi, has built a Hindu temple in Fort Myers, Florida. Her knowledge of temple architecture, sculpture, Indian music, and ancient Hindu rituals is only matched by her love for and expertise in treating children as a pediatrician. My conversations with both of them are always fruitful and fun. Their children, my niece and nephew Nithya and Arvind, are my pride and joy.

My friends Shailaja and Jayashankar and their daughters Madhura and Durga are great raconteurs who shared many stories about how intertwined cows are with the Indian ethos.

In Bangalore, our life has been enriched by Manish and Kavita Sabharwal and their author evenings; Sujata Kelkar Shetty and her Frangipani book club; Shruthi Shetty and her Salon of Ideas; Sejal Shah Gulati and her wine evenings; Stanley Pinto and his Bangalore Black Tie; Ananth and Sandhya Narayanan and their dinners; Devesh Agarwal and his TWC club; Phyllis Fang and Eric Savage and their Ivy Club; Nitin Pai and Pavan Srinath of the Takshashila Institution, amongst others.

Nandan and Rohini Nilekani took us into their home and introduced us to an ever-expanding group of friends. They showed us Coonoor in a way that is hard to replicate. Rohini sent me articles and ideas about cows—animals that she, too, loves.

I also thank Bharati and Jacob, Anuja and Bobby, Rasil and Anurag, and Asha Rai, for their arguments and ideas.

My building features in this book. My wonderful neighbors have all given me ideas that have made their way into my writings. I particularly thank Sumi Cherian who has been my co-conspirator in many cow-related experiments.

THINKING UP AN IDEA is one thing. But the long endeavor of writing a book requires a full supporting cast.

Michelle Tessler, my wonderful agent, was enthusiastic about this project from the start. She has been a fantastic guide and champion of the book.

Amy Gash, the book's editor, has an amazing eye—not just for details, but for flow, rhythm, style, and relevance. Her instincts as a passionate reader have vastly improved this book. Her edits, always imbued with, dare I say, bovine compassion and wry New York humor have made the process interesting and educative. Thank you, Amy.

As always, my parents, Padma and V. R. Narayanaswamy, are my source of strength, character, and ideas. They are my foundation and North Star, giving guidance and direction.

My in-laws, Padma and the late, great V. Ramachandran, are phenomenal role models who set an example simply by the way they live life. I aspire to be like them and have benefited from their sage counsel in all areas of my life, including this book. My mother-in-law, Padma, read through this book, and has always been my most enthusiastic supporter.

Brunson Hoole and Matthew Somoroff have an eye and ear for the English language that I envy. Their meticulous work on this book has made it read "a thousand times better," as my daughters would say.

My greatest thanks go to my husband. He is the brightest man I know, and as a result, I am never bored in our marriage. Our daily conversations enrich my mind and lay the ground for my columns and essays. He gives me newspaper articles, enables my work by giving me coverage at home, and is a terrific father, son, brother, and husband. Most of all, he is the fountainhead of my ideas, and my source of strength and stability.

This book is dedicated to my children.

Ranjini and Malini: dream catchers, heart snatchers, daughters mine. What can I say? With all my love . . . forever and ever . . . To infinity and beyond.

Mani, Vettam. *Puranic Encyclopaedia: A Comprehensive Work with Special Reference to the Epic and Puranic Literature.* 1st English ed. Delhi: Motilal Banarasidas, 1975. (Freely available at archive.org.)

Romero, Irene Gallego, et al. "Herders of Indian and European Cattle Share Their Predominant Allele for Lactase Persistence." *Molecular Biology and Evolution* 29, no. 1 (2012): 249–260.

Said, Edward W. *Reflections on Exile and Other Essays.* Cambridge, MA: Harvard University Press, 2000.

Salque, Mélanie, Peter I. Bogucki, Joanna Pyzel, Iwona Sobkowiak-Tabaka, Ryszard Grygiel, Marzena Szmyt, and Richard P. Evershed. "Earliest Evidence for Cheese Making in the Sixth Millennium BC in Northern Europe." *Nature* 493 (2013): 522–525. doi:10.1038 /nature11698

Sharma, B. V. V. S. R. *The Study of Cow in Sanskrit Literature.* Delhi: GDK Publications, 1980. 68–69.

Sherratt, Andrew. *Plough and Pastoralism: Aspects of the Secondary Product Revolution.* Cambridge: Cambridge University Press, 1981.

Some Aspects of Ancient Indian Culture. Sir William Meyer Lectures, 1938–39. University of Madras, 1940.

Zeder, Melinda A. "Pathways to Animal Domestication." In *Biodiversity in Agriculture: Domestication, Evolution, and Sustainability*, edited by Paul Gepts, Thomas R. Famula, Robert L. Bettinger, Stephen B. Brush, Ardeshir B. Damania, Patrick E. McGuire, and Calvin O. Qualset, 227–259. Cambridge: Cambridge University Press, 2012.

SELECTED READING

Ambedkar, B. R. "Did the Hindus Never Eat Beef?" In *The Untouchables: Who Were They and Why They Became Untouchables?* New Delhi: Amrit, 1948.

Bhandarkar, D. R., Ruth Bollongino, Joachim Burger, Adam Powell, Marjan Mashkour, Jean-Denis Vigne, and Mark G. Thomas. "Modern Taurine Cattle Descended from Small Number of Near-Eastern Founders." *Molecular Biology and Evolution* 29, no. 9 (2012): 2101–2104.

Chakravarti, Mahadev. "Beef-Eating in Ancient India." *Social Scientist* 7, no. 11 (June 1979): 51–55.

Dutt, Manmatha Nath, ed. *The Garuda Puranam.* Calcutta: Society for the Resuscitation of Indian Literature, 1908.

Eggeling, Julius, ed. and trans. *The Satapatha Brahmana*, pt. 2, bks. 3 and 4. Oxford: Clarendon Press, 1885.

Houben, Jan E. M., and Karel R. van Kooij, eds. *Violence Denied: Violence, Non-Violence and the Rationalization of Violence in South Asian Cultural History.* Leiden: Brill, 1999.

Joshi, Sopan. "Why Is the Cow a Political Animal?" *Yahoo! News*, May 12, 2015, https://in.news.yahoo.com/why-is-the-cow-a-political-animal-110119929.html.

Laron, Greger, and Dorian Q. Fuller. "The Evolution of Animal Domestication." *Annual Review of Ecology, Evolution, and Systematics* 45, no. 1 (2014): 115–136.